The Perversion of Holocaust Memory

The Perversion of Holocaust Memory

Writing and Rewriting the Past after 1989

Judith M. Hughes

BLOOMSBURY ACADEMIC
LONDON • NEW YORK • OXFORD • NEW DELHI • SYDNEY

BLOOMSBURY ACADEMIC
Bloomsbury Publishing Plc
50 Bedford Square, London, WC1B 3DP, UK
1385 Broadway, New York, NY 10018, USA
29 Earlsfort Terrace, Dublin 2, Ireland

BLOOMSBURY, BLOOMSBURY ACADEMIC and the Diana logo are trademarks of Bloomsbury Publishing Plc

First published in Great Britain 2022
Paperback edition first published 2023

Copyright © Judith M. Hughes, 2022

Judith M. Hughes has asserted their right under the Copyright, Designs and Patents Act, 1988, to be identified as Author of this work.

Cover image: The Holocaust Memorial, Berlin, Germany.
(© Sean Gallup / Staff / Getty Images)

All rights reserved. No part of this publication may be reproduced or transmitted in any form or by any means, electronic or mechanical, including photocopying, recording, or any information storage or retrieval system, without prior permission in writing from the publishers.

Bloomsbury Publishing Plc does not have any control over, or responsibility for, any third-party websites referred to or in this book. All internet addresses given in this book were correct at the time of going to press. The author and publisher regret any inconvenience caused if addresses have changed or sites have ceased to exist, but can accept no responsibility for any such changes.

Every effort has been made to trace the copyright holders and obtain permission to reproduce the copyright material. Please do get in touch with any enquiries or any information relating to such material or the rights holder. We would be pleased to rectify any omissions in subsequent editions of this publication should they be drawn to our attention.

A catalogue record for this book is available from the British Library.

A catalog record for this book is available from the Library of Congress.

ISBN:	HB:	978-1-3502-8187-5
	PB:	978-1-3502-8191-2
	ePDF:	978-1-3502-8188-2
	eBook:	978-1-3502-8189-9

Typeset by Integra Software Services Pvt. Ltd.

To find out more about our authors and books visit www.bloomsbury.com and sign up for our newsletters.

In memory of my father, Sanford H. Markham

Also by Judith M. Hughes:

To the Maginot Line: The Politics of French Military Preparation in the 1920's (1971)

Emotion and High Politics: Personal Relations at the Summit in Late Nineteenth-Century Britain and Germany (1983)

Reshaping the Psychoanalytic Domain: The Work of Melanie Klein, W.R.D. Fairbairn, and D. W. Winnicott (1989)

From Freud's Consulting Room: The Unconscious in a Scientific Age (1994)

Freudian Analysts/Feminist Issues (1999)

From Obstacle to Ally: The Evolution of Psychoanalytic Practice (2004)

Guilt and Its Vicissitudes: Psychoanalytic Reflections on Morality (2008)

The Holocaust and the Revival of Psychological History (2015)

Witnessing the Holocaust: Six Literary Testimonies (2018)

Contents

Preface	viii
Introduction	1
1 The Papon Affair	5
I. From Barbie and Touvier to Papon	7
II. Excavating France's Colonial Past	12
III. Un Crime de Bureau	16
IV. Coda	23
2 Germans in the Dock	25
I. Willing Executioners	26
II. Crimes of the Wehrmacht	36
III. Coda	43
3 Victims, Jewish and German	45
I. Creating a Memorial	47
II. German Suffering Revisited	54
III. Coda	62
4 From Holodomor to Holocaust	65
I. The *Historikerstreit*	66
II. Variations on a Theme	70
III. Coda	82
5 Revising History, Reviving Nationalism	85
I. Denying Hungary's Past	87
II. Defending Poland's Honor	95
III. Coda	102
Conclusion	105
Notes	107
Select Bibliography	128
Index	142

Preface

This is the third book that I have written about the Holocaust. Only late in my teaching career did I feel able to contain my fright and offer an undergraduate seminar on the subject. By then I had spent well over a decade in a second profession, that of psychoanalyst. So it was to be expected that I would approach the Holocaust by way of what I took to be a renewed interest in the psychological, that is, asking questions about actors' meanings, intentions, and purposes. The book that grew out of that seminar, *The Holocaust and the Revival of Psychological History*, fastened on a handful of historians who grappled with those complicit in genocide. When I undertook a second project—which like the first, though in a roundabout way, grew out of the same undergraduate seminar—I focused on memoirs of survivors. I say roundabout because the last couple of times I taught the seminar, I had the impression, at least in the beginning, that the students took the horrors as a matter of course, suggesting that in war, bad stuff happens. I wanted my seminar and my book, *Witnessing the Holocaust: Six Literary Testimonies*, to shake them up.

By the time I stopped teaching, I assumed that we had reached a shared understanding, of the strangeness, of the moral rupture, of the Holocaust—argued most convincingly by Saul Friedländer in his *Nazi Germany and the Jews*. Timothy Snyder's *Bloodlands*, published only three years after Friedländer's second volume, showed me that I was mistaken. My new book has been prompted by reflections—and distress—at recent efforts to minimize the Holocaust and to play down the anti-Semitism that lay at its root.

In the conclusion to *Witnessing the Holocaust*, I wrote that "for people of my age who were children in the immediate aftermath of the Second World War, knowledge of the Holocaust helped shape our political consciousness and orientation to the world." My aim here is to resist, as forcefully as I can, the efforts to turn a blind eye to that knowledge.

* * * * * * * * * * *

I am grateful to the Academic Senate of the University of California, San Diego for financial support that allowed me to travel to Berlin, Gdansk, Warsaw, and Budapest. In the final stages, anonymous reviewers for Bloomsbury made helpful suggestions.

Along the way, I have found ready listeners and willing readers. I would like to thank Frank Biess, Donald L. Kripke, Edward N. Lee, Ivan Major, Patrick Hyder Patterson, and Stephen A. Schuker. And my son, David, read the manuscript with great care and spotted passages that might bewilder a nonspecialist. It is a pleasure to acknowledge him.

Introduction

In 2005, the historian and public intellectual Tony Judt wrote that Holocaust recognition stood as the "entry ticket" into contemporary Europe. "Those who would become full Europeans in the dawn of the twenty-first century must first assume a new and ... oppressive heritage." For East European countries seeking membership in the European Union, official acknowledgment of the sufferings inflicted on their nation's Jews, including victimization by compatriots, was crucial. And in Western Europe, to minimize the Holocaust was to place oneself beyond the pale of civilized public discourse. "As Europe ... [prepared] to leave World War Two behind," Judt continued, "the recovered memory of Europe's dead Jews ... [had] become the very definition and guarantee of the continent's restored humanity."[1]

Fifteen years later, the landscape looks very different. In France, Marine Le Pen, leader of the far-right Front National, advanced to the second round run-off in the 2017 presidential election; in Germany, that same year, the right-wing Alternative für Deutschland emerged as the third largest party; in Hungary, Viktor Orbán has made his country into a model for "illiberal democracy"; and in Poland, it has become a crime to speak of Polish complicity in the extermination of Jews.

The obvious starting point for my study is 1989—the fall of the Berlin Wall. Postwar Communist authorities had used antifascism to advertise their commitment to peace and democracy—and sanitize their history. Anti-Semitism, in this rendering, was a "political tactic used by the capitalist classes to distract workers from their revolutionary goals." Simply because they lived in a state that was reliably antifascist, citizens in Poland and Hungary had no need to examine their own complicity or involvement in the Holocaust. "The past was not dead. But its ghosts haunted the capitalist West, not the socialist East."[2]

As for Germany, as long as it was divided, guilt for National Socialism could be passed back and forth over the German-German border. East Germany, as a communist state, identified capitalism as the source of fascism and drew comparisons between West Germany and the Third Reich. For its part, West Germany pointed to totalitarianism as the common feature of both fascism and communism and vilified East Germany as the communist equivalent of National Socialism. The result: neither state came to terms with its Nazi past. When Germany was unified in 1990, this ritual of buck-passing and self-exoneration became obsolete. Unification meant that the game playing would have to stop, sooner or later.[3]

In the 1990s, France, as well, was still coping with the aftermath of the 1940s. Even though French historians—following in the wake of their foreign colleagues—had established beyond question the overwhelming responsibility of France's wartime rulers for the deportation of Jews from French soil, the official line never varied: whatever was done under or by the Vichy regime was the affair of Vichy. Vichy was not "France"; it was an authoritarian parenthesis in the history of the French republic. Thus, France's public conscience remained unblemished.[4]

The silence that had been enforced for decades was finally broken with a series of trials—most dramatically that of Maurice Papon in 1997–8. This is what I take up in the first chapter. A French court proved willing to pass judgment on a Vichy official who had had a successful postwar career as public servant and politician. Papon could not hide behind procedures any more than soldiers could hide behind orders. Bureaucrats, the court ruled, even if acting in accordance with administrative policy, still had to answer personally for their actions.

In Chapter 2, I move on to Germany. The publication of Daniel Jonah Goldhagen's book *Hitler's Willing Executioners* and the *Vernichtungskrieg* (*War of Annihilation*) Exhibition, both in the mid-1990s, brought home to the German people the full extent of their parents' and grandparents' participation in the Final Solution. For decades, culpability had been carefully circumscribed. Now it was assigned far and wide throughout the Third Reich—with the Wehrmacht very much included. The events recounted in these first two chapters—by and large success stories—buttressed confidence that the memory of the Holocaust had become fixed in the consciousness of West Europeans.

In Chapter 3, it becomes clear that such confidence was unwarranted—despite the fact that plans to build a major Berlin memorial specifically to Jews murdered in the Holocaust were realized. Here was a clear commitment to Jewish victims. At just about the same time, Jörg Friedrich published *Der Brand* (*The Fire*), which brought renewed attention to the Allied bombing campaign that had laid waste to German cities. Friedrich's likening British and American destruction of Germany's architectural treasures to Nazi efforts to erase not only the Jews themselves but their cultural legacy—his equating of German and Jewish suffering—was perverse.

In Chapter 4, I look at two authors, a generation apart, who shifted the focus—perversely—from Germany and anti-Semitism to the Soviet Union and communism. Ernst Nolte, in the late 1980s, insisted that Nazi genocide was a response to Bolshevik violence. Timothy Snyder, in 2010, echoing Nolte's anti-Soviet animus, claimed that the war against the Jews followed from the failure of the war against the Soviets. Where Saul Friedländer in his magisterial *Nazi Germany and the Jews*[5]—a less celebrated, yet more nuanced, account than Goldhagen's[6]—pointed to anti-Semitism as the driving force behind the Holocaust, Nolte and Snyder marginalized it. Nolte's arguments raised the hackles of German historians; Snyder's book won prestigious prizes. However, it was not in Germany nor in France, but in Eastern Europe, particularly in Poland, that his work met with the warmest reception. Was it because he demanded no conscience-searching from East Europeans?

Snyder's portrayal of the populations of Eastern Europe as victimized by two totalitarian powers fit with narratives that found favor in Hungary and Poland. In Chapter 5, I focus on these two countries. In both, populist leaders managed to avoid a frank reckoning with their country's wartime treatment of Jews. They side-stepped inconvenient facts: that without the active participation of homegrown perpetrators, the Holocaust would never have reached the proportions it did. They tried to cover up the truth, to keep silent about what had happened. And this persistence in error has gone along with trafficking in anti-Semitic rhetoric.[7]

I have used the word "perverse" a couple of times. What do I mean by it? The four countries I study could all claim to be victims of Nazi Germany or the Allies or both Nazi Germany and the Communist Soviet Union. But they—or many of their countrymen—were also perpetrators. It is this complexity that has proved so hard to tolerate. It is as if one could not be a victim and a perpetrator at the same time. The victim position, because of its avoidance—or really denial—of guilt and remorse, amounts to a radical simplification. And it is often preferred. What I am suggesting is that this denial, a determined turning away from the truth, is both perverse and not uncommon.

In recent years, Holocaust remembrance has been caught in the backlash to the refugee crisis—with its revival of ethno-nationalism and violation of democratic norms. Where will it lead?[8] In expanding the European Union, politicians had assumed that the nations of the former Soviet Empire would follow a path charted by the West; they now find their own liberal values called into question.

1

The Papon Affair

On July 16, 1995, Jacques Chirac, France's President, gave a speech marking the anniversary of the massive Vél d'Hiv roundups—in July 1942, French police arrested 13,152 Jewish men, women, and children in Paris, interning the majority under appalling conditions in the Vélodrome d'Hiver bicycle stadium before shipping them to Auschwitz. In speaking at the annual ceremony, the first President of the Republic to do so, Chirac "used a language free of the ambiguities, loopholes, and contortions that until then characterized most presidential speeches" touching on the Vichy regime.[1] He underlined the responsibility of the state: it was French police agents who carried out the arrests of Jews, who first penned up their prisoners in French camps, and who then deported them on French trains. The principle of state continuity, especially in a country as centralized as France, entails, he claimed, assuming responsibility for acts carried out under the authority of its leaders, even if those leaders were responding to Nazi demands. Here was a stark condemnation of the state, the rulers, the higher echelons, and of government employees who committed crimes or let crimes be committed.

At the war's end the French had punished the most visible Nazi collaborators: 9,000 were summarily executed during the liberation campaign, 1,000 were executed after a trial, and 40,000 were sentenced to prison.[2] Those claiming to have worked for the Resistance—and indeed the postwar government fostered the myth that nearly all French citizens had supported the Resistance—were spared; and civil servants and businessmen, desperately needed by the new government to revive the crippled nation, were among those who escaped unscathed. It took a quarter century for this myth to be seriously challenged: in late 1969, *The Sorrow and the Pity*, a documentary by Marcel Orphuls, portrayed a France more collaborationist than resistant; in 1972, Robert O. Paxton's *Vichy France: Old Guard and New Order, 1940-1944* showed that Vichy never engaged in any kind of subterfuge, that it had begged the Germans to accept collaboration, and had done so starting in the summer of 1940.[3] Even so, French leaders dragged their feet in bringing Vichy officials to account. For example, in the early 1990s, President François Mitterand intervened to postpone the trial of his friend René Bousquet, the police chief most responsible for French assistance to the Nazis. Chirac's speech, delivered by someone who was only twelve years old in 1944, served to speed up the machinery of justice. Two years later Maurice Papon stood trial for crimes against humanity.

Who was Papon? He figured as the embodiment of administrative continuity between Vichy and successive postwar governments. Radical under Léon Blum, Pétainist under Vichy, socialist during the Fourth Republic (1946–58), Gaullist then Giscardist under the Fifth (1958–present), Papon seemed less committed to the republican government than to serving the state, whoever was in power and whatever the nature of the regime. Among the posts he held was Paris chief of police in the Fifth Republic. He subsequently moved on to a political career becoming a Gaullist representative in the National Assembly and finally budget minister under Raymond Barre during the Giscard presidency.

A Vichy functionary, but only of a middling sort. So why Papon? Two others had been accused of crimes against humanity, Jean Leguay, Bousquet's representative in the occupied zone and Bousquet himself. Leguay was on the verge of standing trial when he died in 1989. Four years later, Bousquet, the man responsible for the Vél d'Hiv roundup, was gunned down in his apartment building and thus escaped judicial reckoning. As for Papon's immediate superior, Maurice Sabatier, he died before charges could be brought against him. Papon, it turned out, had the disadvantage of a long life.

The 1997 trial lasted six months, the longest in French legal history, and ended with Papon's conviction for complicity in crimes against humanity. He had stood accused of lending active assistance to arrests, internments, and deportations as the Germans pursued, on French soil, their project of exterminating Jews. Close to 1,600 Jews were deported in ten convoys from the Bordeaux region to Drancy and from there to Auschwitz; Papon was implicated in eight of these. A reporter for *Le Monde* summed up the prosecution's case: "He signed what he should not have signed, he carried out what he should not have carried out, and, above all, he organized what he should not have organized."[4]

At the start of the trial, a battalion of lawyers, broadcasters, journalists, and historians descended on Bordeaux. Video cameras were installed on the four walls of the courtroom to record, for posterity, each moment of the trial. During recesses, as the lawyers exited, television crews waited for them in the hallway. In front of the cameras, they described what had been going on and added their particular spin. And outside the courthouse, protests, vigils, and readings of the names of French Holocaust victims took place throughout the trial. With this kind of saturated media and public attention, expectations ran high that the trial would yield lessons for French society as a whole.

I. From Barbie and Touvier to Papon

As the Second World War drew to a close, the Allies debated how to punish the Nazi elite. The British, Churchill chief among them, toyed with the idea of simply executing a dozen or so leading figures. Stalin increased the number: he suggested shooting 50,000 German general staff officers. The Americans took a different line: senior figures in the War Department argued that a legal response offered a valuable opportunity to apply and enforce principles of international law. And to extend them as well.

In May 1945, Harry Truman—he had become president a month earlier following Roosevelt's death—appointed Robert Jackson to lead the prosecution team in the trial of major German war criminals. During a long summer, the representatives of Great Britain, France, the Soviet Union, and the United States hammered out a charter. Of all the difficulties, the most serious concerned Article 6, the list of crimes with which to charge the defendants. Seeking help, Jackson turned to Hersch Lauterpacht, a British legal expert. It was Lauterpacht's proposal to put a new term into the Nuremberg statute to address atrocities against civilians—crimes against humanity.

Here is the exact language:

> Crimes against humanity: namely, murder, extermination, enslavement, deportation, and other inhumane acts committed against any civilian population, before or during the war, or persecutions on political, racial, or religious grounds in execution of or in connection with any crime within the jurisdiction of the [International Military] Tribunal, whether or not in violation of the domestic law of the country where perpetrated.[5]

Clearly this was an innovation, so Lauterpacht told the British Foreign Office. It declared that international law was not only law "between States" but "also the law of mankind." Those who transgressed it, even if they were leaders, would have no immunity. Crimes against humanity thus reflected "the outraged conscience of the world."[6]

As it turned out, crimes against humanity did not stand as the great master offense. At the Nuremberg trial, its radical potential was restricted. The tribunal essentially enfolded crimes against humanity into war crimes, treating them as either a subcategory of war crimes or as offenses covering a small range of conduct not formally covered by conventional rules of war.

The charter of the International Military Tribunal had failed to mention what, if any, statute of limitations would apply to the crimes tried at Nuremberg. In June 1964, French legislators filed a bill making crimes against humanity imprescriptible, that is, not subject to a time limit. (The bill was in response to an announcement by the West German government that, as of May 8, 1965, the statute of limitations would be valid for all war crimes, including crimes against humanity. This action was later postponed.) The discussion in the National Assembly went without a hitch, and in December the bill passed unanimously. The new law covered only crimes against humanity, not war crimes, and in 1967, the French applied the statute of limitations to the latter. It meant that all future prosecution of war criminals would be pursued as crimes against humanity alone.

* * * * * * * * * * * *

On the morning of April 6, 1944, a detachment of the Lyon Gestapo carried out a raid on a children's house in Izieu and arrested all the occupants. For a year the house had provided refuge for dozens of children. Some were French; others had come from Algeria, Belgium, Austria, Germany, and Poland. All were Jewish. The forty-four children, aged between four and sixteen, along with seven staff members, were trucked off, incarcerated in a Lyon prison, deported to Drancy, and from there shipped to Auschwitz. Of those rounded up, only one adult survived.[7] Klaus Barbie, SS Hauptsturmführer (Captain), chief of the Intelligence Section of the Gestapo in Lyon, had signed the deportation order.

Twice in the 1950s, Barbie was tried and sentenced to death. Both times *in absentia*. In 1952, a permanent military tribunal in Lyon convicted him of war crimes, and in 1954, he was again convicted of different war crimes in a different region of France. His crimes included assassinations, arson, and pillage. Above all, he was notorious as the alleged torturer and killer of Jean Moulin, hero of the French Resistance.

In 1945, the Allies had placed Barbie's name on a list of war criminals. In no small measure, thanks to going to work for the U.S. Army's Counter-Intelligence Corps in Germany, he was able to escape. When the French discovered his whereabouts, he managed, thanks again to the Americans, to make his way to Bolivia. For three decades he lived under the assumed name of Klaus Altmann, all the while conducting business and unapologetically spouting Nazi propaganda. In 1971, the Klarsfelds, indefatigable Nazi hunters, tracked him down. It took another dozen years for the French to ask for, then demand, his extradition.[8] On February 5, 1983, Barbie, now aged seventy, arrived back in France. Marcel Orphuls's documentary *Hotel Terminus* (1988) captures Barbie's changing fortunes and the twists and turns of bringing him to trial.

This time Barbie was charged with crimes against humanity. Who were the victims? The Nuremberg definition described them as "civilian populations." Barbie was accused of having deported 650 people, Jews and Resistance fighters in almost equal number. The Jews were apparently civilians, arrested, deported, and assassinated simply because they had been born. But the Resistance fighters sent to Buchenwald, Dachau, or Mauthausen—who were they? After the war, the French gave them the title of "honorary combatants." As such, their arrest, torture, or inhumane treatment in the Nazi camps fell into the category of war crimes—prescriptible in French law. If, however, one bracketed their character as combatants and instead emphasized the nature of their sufferings, they, too, could be counted among the victims of crimes against humanity. In the end the High Court of Appeals did just that: it expanded the definition of victims of crimes against humanity to include Resistance fighters as well as Jews.[9]

As the legal scholar Lawrence Douglas put it, at Nuremberg, "the Jew was treated as a kind of lesser political prisoner, a victim of a novel species of war crime; at the Barbie trial, the Resistance member was treated as an innocent martyr, a kind of Jew, slaughtered for his membership in a reviled group."[10]

The trial lasted from May 11 to July 4, 1987. The court rendered a guilty verdict, and sentenced Barbie to life imprisonment.

* * * * * * * * * * * *

"Klaus Barbie was to the SS, what Paul Touvier was to the Milice,"—Vichy's brutal paramilitary force. Lawyers accusing Touvier of crimes against humanity repeated this refrain again and again. On the surface the comparison seemed a good one. Barbie, chief of the Gestapo's intelligence section in Lyon, was assigned to pursue Resistance members and to organize the mass murder of the Jews. Touvier, regional chief of the intelligence service of the Milice, also in Lyon, gathered information on members of the Resistance and hunted them down. Ferreting out Jews was also one of his specialties. Finally, their crimes were committed only a few dozen kilometers apart, at Izieu and Rilleux, both located in the same department of the Ain.

The lawyers also compared Barbie and Touvier's crimes. But the comparison was far from persuasive. At Izieu, at a house way out in the middle of the mountains, Barbie came to take hidden children. The sole "justification" for this act was a plan for the systematic extermination of Jews—wherever they might be. The roundup had been premeditated long in advance and was driven by a fierce ideological determination to kill Jews. In contrast, Touvier arrested certain specific Jewish individuals—all men—with the aim of seeking vengeance for the killing of Philippe Henriot, Minister of Information and voice of Radio Vichy. The seven victims were murdered and left where they fell, as an example to terrorize the population. Unlike Izieu, these executions did not stand as a textbook example of the Final Solution.

Twice in the aftermath of the war, Touvier escaped justice. On September 18, 1946, and again on March 4, 1947, he was charged with treason and sharing intelligence with the enemy. Both times he was condemned to death *in absentia*. On the lam within France, Touvier married secretly and had two children; he survived financially thanks to the complicity of powerful figures in the Catholic Church. By 1967 the statute of limitations had run out on the convictions themselves. There were, however, "secondary" penalties, for example, the confiscation of property. In 1971, after years of effort by a prelate devoted to his cause, Touvier obtained a pardon from President Georges Pompidou. News of the pardon provoked an uproar, and Touvier was forced to go into hiding once again. For the most part he holed up in right-wing monasteries. On May 24, 1989, gendarmes located him at the Saint-François priory in Nice. This time he was accused of crimes against humanity.[11]

Before the case came to trial, the original indictment was thrown out. In April 1992, the Indicting Chamber of the Paris Court of Appeals dismissed the charges.[12] In the Barbie case, the High Court of Appeals had restricted the "inhumane acts and persecutions" constituting crimes against humanity to those "committed in the name of a state practicing a politics of ideological hegemony."[13] Now the Indicting Chamber justified its decision by claiming that "no well-defined ideology ruled" at Vichy, that for Vichy Jews were not considered to be "enemies of the State" as they were in Germany, and that the phrase "state practicing a politics of ideological hegemony" applied to Hitler's Third Reich, but not to Pétain's regime—Vichy was described as a "constellation of good intentions and political animosities."[14]

Later that same year, the High Court of Appeals partially nullified this decision.[15] The murders at Rilleux, the High Court claimed, were committed by order of the Gestapo, an organization belonging to a state practicing a politics of ideological hegemony. So the trial, which finally took place in the spring of 1994, hinged on whether or not Touvier had been an accomplice of the Germans. If he had acted alone, on his own initiative, or on the initiative of the Milice, or even that of the Vichy government, he would have been acquitted.[16]

That Touvier remained frozen in the past became clear in the courtroom reading of the famous "green notebook," a secret notebook in which, between 1985 and 1988, he expressed his longstanding beliefs: he was still an ardent defender of Vichy and the Milice; still a vicious and unrepentant anti-Semite; and he still denounced politicians as "kikes" and wrote of Jewish conspiracies and cabals. The telling effect of the reading was "less in the display of Touvier's undying hatred (that was expected) than in the immediate and dramatic proof of the enormous lies he put forth throughout the court sessions: 'I have never been an anti-Semite!' To which the presiding judge ... never tired of repeating. 'Only the accused has the right to lie.'"[17] [True in the French legal system, not in the American.]

It was on the basis of a lie that Touvier was convicted of complicity in a crime against humanity and sentenced to life in prison. During the preliminary investigation, Touvier had claimed, falsely, that he had acted in compliance with German orders. For the prosecution it had been crucial to block all attempts by the defense to hide behind "pressure of the occupying force." And the preliminary investigation had demonstrated that though the Germans had no objection to the reprisal following Henriot's death—it did, after all, fit right into the logic of Nazi policy—they had not gotten involved. With the ruling of the High Court of Appeals, the case was turned upside down. Suddenly the prosecution had to prove that Touvier had indeed acted at the instigation of the Germans—using the same witnesses and documents it had used to make the opposite argument. It was thus necessary to accept Touvier's earlier declarations—that he had been acting under German orders—as essentially truthful. It was thus necessary to accept his lie.[18]

The legal framework of the case meant that the court was obliged to turn a deaf ear to those who were demanding that the anti-Semitic aspects of Vichy or, at the very least, that the anti-Semitism of the Milice should be put on trial. The Touvier trial could not be a trial of Vichy or more precisely of Vichy's anti-Semitic policy.

* * * * * * * * * * *

On October 20, 1942, four armed police officers, two French, two German, arrived at the Slitinsky's home in Bordeaux. They had come to arrest the

Slitinskys as part of a larger operation during which Jews in the Bordeaux region were to be seized, interned, and their property confiscated. Michel Slitinsky, then seventeen years old, managed to escape. His father and sister were not so lucky. They were deported to Auschwitz, where the father was murdered.

In May 1981, between the two rounds of the presidential election that would see Mitterand's victory over Giscard, *Le Canard enchaîné* published documents bearing Papon's signature that implicated him in the arrest of the Slitinskys. Papon, at the time budget minister, was at the apogee of a long and distinguished career. Slitinsky, as well as other victims or their surviving relatives, filed criminal charges against him. (In French law, private citizens as well as the state may initiate criminal proceedings.) Since the statute of limitations had already run out on war crimes, the only option available to the civil parties was to accuse Papon of committing a crime against humanity.

Further legal tinkering was required. In a pretrial appeal, Papon argued that his acts did not constitute complicity in crimes against humanity because there was no proof that he adhered to the "hegemonic political ideology" of the Nazis. Ultimately the High Court of Appeals held that an accomplice to crimes against humanity need not subscribe to the ideology of the principal culprits. Rather it sufficed that he knowingly facilitated the preparation or consummation of the crime. From a prosecutorial standpoint, this ruling was fortunate indeed. Had the High Court held that the state had to prove that each perpetrator or accomplice concurred in the belief system that led to crimes against humanity, it would have wreaked havoc with the effort to bring Papon to trial.[19]

If Papon had been tried at the beginning of the 1980s after *Le Canard enchaîné* had revealed the reality of his role during the war, it is safe to say that he would have been acquitted. It was crucial to proceed step by step if the public, as well as the judiciary, were to accept that the perpetrators of crimes against humanity, or their accomplices, could be Vichy officials.

II. Excavating France's Colonial Past

It is customary in French courts for a trial to open with a sketch of the defendant's biography. Within a week of the start—the trial began on October 8, 1997—Papon's role as a government functionary in France's North African possessions came up for review. Between the end of the war and his taking over as prefect of police in 1958, Papon served three stints in North Africa. His first posting, in 1949, took him to Constantine. For two years he served as prefect of the region, the largest, in terms of land area, and the poorest in French Algeria. His second posting, in 1954, found him in the protectorate of Morocco. Placed in charge of police operations, he displayed his usual zeal, that is, rigorous suppression of native "terrorists," including roundups and detention. With scarcely an interruption, his third posting, in 1956, found him again in Algeria, now at war. As inspector-general of administration on a special mission to Constantine, he did not hesitate to order a crackdown. By the end of his first year back in the Constantinois, "the forces of order had exacted quite a toll on the native population: 4,200 rebels killed, 226 wounded, 401 captured, and more than 1,000 weapons seized."[20]

By 1958, the Algerian War had moved to the mainland, and a strongman seemed to be what the situation required. So months before de Gaulle's return to power, Papon was recalled to Paris to serve as prefect of police. He quickly inaugurated repressive measures against Algerians living in the city: police searches, roundups, detentions, and interrogations, including water torture, impaling on bottles, and electric shocks—all of which had been previously used in Algeria, all of which set the stage for the events of October 1961.

* * * * * * * * * * *

On the evening of October 17, 1961, a peaceful demonstration of 30,000 Algerian immigrants, organized by the Front Libération Nationale (FLN), converged on central Paris. It was met by police violence: at least fifty—and possibly as many as 200—Algerians were murdered that night and another 11,538 men were savagely beaten and herded into sports stadiums.[21]

Tensions had been building over the previous summer: peace negotiations between the Algerian Provisional Government and the French had broken down; assassinations of police officers in Paris had resumed—between late August and early October eleven officers were killed and seventeen wounded. On October 5, "to combat terrorism," Papon imposed a curfew from 8:30 p.m. to 5:30 a.m. on Algerians. The huge mobilization of October 17 was planned—and planned meticulously—as a protest. Those marching were to carry no weapons; the men were to wear their Sunday best, and the presence of women and children served as a guarantee of benign intent. What the organizers got horribly wrong was the capacity of the police for "extra-legal" violence—violence that was "indirectly but knowingly facilitated by the government at the highest level."[22]

Facilitated by the government, how? In early September, a new phase of sinister and murderous repression of the FLN began. Even moderate police officers of the major union talked of forming commandos that would take matters into their own hands; almost daily North Africans who had been arrested by the police were later found dead in the Seine or in the canals of Paris. At this juncture, Papon deliberately encouraged the blood-thirstiness. On October 2, during a round of inspecting local police stations, he made it perfectly clear that "he would use his authority to ensure that the police would be '*couvert*' or protected for any actions they might take against Algerians, a term that was widely understood by the rank and file to give a green light to the most violent forms of action."[23] Knowing that they would be "covered" by Papon, the police ran amok.

After the massacre, what concerned Papon was less the scale of the carnage than the fact that it had not been properly concealed and thus opened the way to a potential political scandal. He need not have worried. Within six months, the massacre had been successfully erased from public memory. Not until 1997, was the man who had seen more than 11,000 Algerians arrested and bused away to be maltreated and, in some cases, killed, put on trial—for having handed Jews over to the Germans.

* * * * * * * * * * *

For how long can a man be considered to be his same old self? This question recurred throughout the trial. At age eighty-seven, Papon appeared a man of authority, in full possession of his faculties, proud and haughty. In addressing the court, in outlining his biography, his parents, his childhood, his studies, his entrance into government administration, his military service, he took his time, spoke easily, choosing the right tense, the right word. From the outset, observers understood that here was someone well able to defend himself.[24]

During the session of October 15, Papon rose to state his case—or, rather, to launch a counter-offensive. Not one of the deaths, he insisted, could be laid at the door of the prefecture of police. How, then, he asked, could it happen that Algerians were thrown into the Seine? The bodies that were recovered, the identifications that were made, proved that the victims were dissidents from the FLN. It was FLN commandos who had done away with their opponents and, afterwards, blamed the police. When questioned about published reports of witnesses who told of brutality, violence, assassination, Papon replied, in effect, that one couldn't trust the media.[25]

The following day it was the turn of Jean-Luc Einaudi, author of the authoritative *La Bataille de Paris*, published in 1991, to take the stand and give a full account of what had happened that night. No—Algerians were not killing Algerians. An example: marchers moving along the Boulevard Bonne-Nouvelle, going from the Place de la République toward the Opéra, were attacked without warning in front of the Rex Theatre. This episode was one of the bloodiest: protesters were shot and beaten to death. Throughout the city, thousands were rounded up. Because police vehicles did not suffice, Papon requisitioned city buses—they returned covered with blood. When those rounded up, already wounded, arrived at designated sports stadiums—also requisitioned—they were met by welcoming committees: double rows of policemen beat them mercilessly, aiming at their heads and genitals. The sanitation corps of the army, coming later to clean up, found frightful scenes.

As for Papon's personal responsibility, Einaudi elaborated: he was at the command center of the prefecture of police; whatever was happening could not escape his knowledge. It was one thing to question the demonstrators, and another to fire on them, and something else again to throw them into the Seine. It was one thing to arrest people and something else to murder them in detention facilities. The order given to Papon by his superiors was that there be no demonstration, not that there should be fatalities.[26]

Klarsfeld *fils*, Arno, a lawyer for the plaintiffs, interjected: the accused has the habit of shifting responsibility for his deeds onto others. And here he was at it again: this time claiming that it was Algerians who assassinated Algerians.[27]

* * * * * * * * * * *

Months after Einaudi testified, Papon sued him for defamation. On March 26, 1999, the Seventeenth Chamber of the Paris Correctional Tribunal handed down its verdict. The judge read the thirty-one page decision; the audience held its breath. The court found that Einaudi's research was unquestionably valid; so too his attribution of responsibility to Papon.[28] For close to forty years, these events had been almost completely covered up. Now, one commentator noted, it was like the return of the repressed.[29]

On October 17, 2012, "with three short sentences of recognition" President François Hollande paid homage to those massacred fifty-one years earlier.[30] And on September 13, 2018, his successor, Emmanuel Macron, released a statement in which he admitted what no French president before him had dared to acknowledge: that torture by French forces was widespread during the Algerian War and that is was, in Macron's words, a product of a "legally established system."[31]

III. Un Crime de Bureau

When historians were called to testify—for both the prosecution and the defense—they appeared not as witnesses in the traditional sense, but to provide perspective.[32] And this was all the more necessary given how much time had elapsed between the commission of the crimes and their being brought to trial. As Paxton, who led off, made clear, he was not a specialist on Bordeaux nor on Papon's career; he could—and did—sketch the most prominent features of the Vichy regime.[33]

Even before the defeat in 1940, France had experienced a severe anti-refugee backlash. After Hitler's assumption of power, it had become the major haven for German and Central European refugees, the overwhelming majority of whom were Jews. By the summer of 1933, at the height of the first wave of the refugee crisis, France had absorbed some 25,000. The number ebbed in subsequent years, and then, in early 1939, following the Anschluss of Austria, the Munich "appeasement" conference, and the Kristallnacht pogroms, it swelled again. In addition, there were 15,000 to 20,000 illegal East European Jewish refugees—either from Germany or Poland, Romania or Hungary—as well as roughly 500,000 Spanish republicans. Following this influx, French attitudes toward refugees notably hardened. Yet only after the German occupation in 1940 were voices for a more liberal refugee policy effectively silenced.[34]

On June 22, 1940, French delegates signed an armistice with the Third Reich: Alsace and Lorraine were then annexed to Germany; two northeastern departments were placed under the administration of a German military governor based in Belgium, and the rest of France—the vast bulk—was divided into occupied and unoccupied zones, separated by a demarcation line that quickly became a formidable barrier, difficult to cross legally and dangerous to cross illegally. About three-fifths of the country north of the Loire and extending south in a narrow strip along the Atlantic coast to the Spanish frontier constituted the occupied zone, administered by a German military governor. About forty departments south of the line were unoccupied. This arrangement lasted until November 11, 1942, when, after the Allied landings in North Africa, the German army occupied the southern zone except for an area east of the Rhone that fell to the Italians. Once the Italians extricated themselves from the war in September 1943, the Germans took control of that area as well. Bordeaux was in the occupied zone.

Within days of signing the armistice, the Third Republic ceased to exist. In mid-May, after the Germans had invaded the Low Countries, Prime Minister

Paul Reynaud invited Marshal Philippe Pétain, the First World War hero of Verdun, to join the cabinet as vice-prime minister. Then on June 16, besieged on all sides by officers and politicians insisting on an armistice, and with the German army already in Paris, Reynaud resigned and urged the president to ask Pétain to form a government. Once the armistice was in place, Pétain summoned senators and deputies, and those who answered his summons—Communists had already been expelled and others had sailed to North Africa—agreed, by an overwhelming majority, to revoke the constitution of the Third Republic and to grant Pétain full powers to promulgate a new one. He thereupon gave himself the title of chief of the French state, claimed responsibility for making and executing all laws, and suspended the Senate and Chamber of Deputies indefinitely.

During the summer and fall of 1940, the French government, now headquartered at Vichy, began a legislative assault on Jews living in France. On July 17, without mentioning Jews, it issued a law limiting employment in the public sector to individuals born of French fathers. On July 22, it restricted opportunities previously enjoyed by naturalized citizens and set up a commission to review all the naturalizations granted since 1927. A law of August 16 established a doctors' guild and limited access to the medical professions to those with French fathers, and a law of September 10 regulated admission to the bar in similar fashion. And then the *Statut des juifs*, issued on October 3, assigned on the basis of race, an inferior position in French law to a whole segment of the population. It "began by defining who was Jewish in the eyes of the French state, and then excluded those Jews from top positions in the public service, from the officer corps and from the ranks of noncommissioned officers, and from professions that influence public opinion: teaching, the press, radio, film, and theater. Jews could hold menial public service positions provided they had served in the French armed forces between 1914 and 1918, or had distinguished themselves in the 1939–40 campaign."[35]

Not since the 1870s had religion been part of vital statistics in France. In September 1941, the Germans ordered a census of Jews in the occupied zone. French police quickly and efficiently registered Jews by name, address, profession, and place of birth. The following summer it was the turn of Jews in the unoccupied zone to be labeled and counted. No Jews were exempt from the obligation to declare themselves—not even those exempt from other laws.[36] For the Germans, the card files, which could be found in every prefecture, proved essential in arrests and roundups, keeping the machinery of extermination running smoothly.

Vichy's anti-Jewish measures—as was the case with all its legislation—covered both occupied and unoccupied zones alike. The summer of 1942 marked a turning point, from a lawmaking stage—forcing Jews out of public service, instituting a *numerus clausus* in professions and higher education, and "aryanizing" the economy—to a stage dominated by police actions—roundups, internment, and deportation. Tasks that the Germans could not accomplish on their own. There were simply not enough of them to do the job. In mid-1942, the German authorities had only three police battalions, roughly 2,500 to 3,000 men at their disposal. Relatively isolated in French society, unfamiliar with the language and the urban and rural landscape where many Jews sought to hide, and frequently hated by the population, the Germans functioned with difficulty even in optimum conditions. In contrast, the French had a powerful police apparatus, firmly under the control of the Ministry of the Interior and its secretary-general, René Bousquet. Eager to protect the appearance of sovereignty, Bousquet reached an agreement with General Karl Oberg, Higher SS and Police Leader. The French were given a free hand in those matters that did not affect German interests; in return the French police promised to act vigorously against enemies of the Reich. The Oberg-Bousquet accords were still being negotiated when the great roundups of July 1942 began.[37]

At the end of 1940, the Jewish population had numbered 330,000, of whom 135,000 were foreign. Between March 27, 1942, and August 12, 1944, approximately 75,000 Jews were deported from France in seventy-four convoys. About 2,800 survived. In addition, at least 1,000 Jews were executed in France during the war and another 3,000 died in internment camps. Roughly 12.6 percent of French Jews, including those naturalized at birth or later, and 41 percent of foreign Jews perished in the Holocaust.[38]

* * * * * * * * * *

A week after Paxton testified, Marc Olivier Baruch, author of *Servir l'État*, took the stand.[39] A high functionary himself, he presented a rich portrait of his Vichy counterparts. Without having to account to legislative bodies, which had been suspended, the functionaries found themselves liberated. But they were not mere technicians. They were political; they were committed to collaboration; for them it was essential to show the Germans that they could be counted on.

They were not anti-Semitic, or not notably so, Baruch claimed. But the prosecutor interjected: "You explain in your work that in the face of certain demands for collaboration, for instance, ... [conscription for labor service in

Germany], these same functionaries knew how, in one way or another, to work around strict obedience." Why did they not do the same when it came to applying measures against Jews? Baruch answered: "It was, at first, a question of foreign Jews—and one shouldn't minimize the part played by xenophobia. When it came to French Jews, it was more complicated." How? Baruch sidestepped the issue, referring simply to latent anti-Semitism, before moving on.[40]

What Baruch—and Paxton as well—was intent on addressing was the room for maneuver of a Vichy official. In 1942, Paxton claimed, it was possible to disobey and cited the example of a general who refused to comply and was simply relieved of his command. Baruch supplied figures: nineteen prefects and twenty-three sub-prefects were removed. (He did not elaborate on what happened to them afterwards.) Papon acknowledged that he could have resigned, and that it would have been easy to do so. But given how he had been brought up, the values instilled in him by parents and teachers, to resign would have been tantamount to desertion. He preferred "to dirty his hands in the frightful collective and individual dramas" of those years.[41] Once the tide turned, Papon, like many Vichy officials, gave discreet help to the Resistance. In 1981, when charges were first filed against him, he asked a "jury of honor" composed of senior Resistance leaders to review his case. It concluded that although he had aided the Resistance, he bore some responsibility for what the prefecture of Bordeaux had done and that he should have resigned in July 1942.

Turning to Papon, the presiding judge posed the crucial question: "Did you know what awaited the Jews who had been deported?" Papon replied: "I didn't know. No more than the Jews themselves …. There were several descriptions circulating of what the policy of 'transfer' meant." We suspected a "cruel fate" but never extermination.[42] Knowing that a "cruel fate" lay in store for the women, children, and elderly whose arrests the prefecture ordered, did not keep Papon from signing the necessary documents.[43]

* * * * * * * * * *

The first convoy left Bordeaux on July 18, 1942, the last on May 13, 1944, just weeks before Allied forces landed in Normandy. From almost the outset, the claim that the Jews were being deported to forced labor camps somewhere in the East made no sense. Why deport children—as happened on August 26, 1942? Why deport the elderly—as happened on May 13, 1944?

Children had been spared in the initial roundup. They had not been included in the first convoy that left Mérignac, an internment camp in the Gironde, for

Drancy on July 18. Then a new order came from the Germans, which the police command in Paris decided must be carried out: children, who in the meantime had been dispersed among guardians in the vicinity of Bordeaux, were to be sent to Drancy to rejoin their parents.[44]

To be sure, Papon had not signed the order, but his office was charged with carrying it out. What did he do? If one were to believe the accused, nothing. He simply transmitted the German order to those who had organized the placement of the children.

The presiding judge intervened: he insisted that Papon clearly indicate the extent of his involvement in the arrest of the youngsters, some of whom were under two years of age. Who located them in the families sheltering them? Who collected them in taxis—the court exhibited invoices for transportation costs? Papon mumbled a response: he didn't give any directives; the Germans had the addresses. The presiding judge persisted. Who gave them the addresses? Who, in the prefecture, was responsible for this dreadful roundup? Papon claimed ignorance.

What Papon could not know, and what one learned only later, was that at the moment the children arrived at Mérignac—by what means remained obscure— and then at Drancy, their parents had already been exterminated. They had been murdered upon arrival in Auschwitz, on August 17 and 18. At the beginning of September, the children suffered the same fate.[45]

With the convoys of 1943, filled with young children, one might have thought that the abomination had reached its limit. The last transfer of May 1944 was something even more terrible. The hospitals were emptied: the bed-ridden, the mutilated, the dying were among those crammed into cattle cars. The majority of deportees were over seventy, some over eighty.

The presiding judge underlined the efficiency of French authorities. Intent on making sure where the Jews were, the prefecture had requested of all arrondissements—and received within forty-eight hours—an updating of the card files, taking account of address changes, disappearances, for both sexes, for all ages and all nationalities. However the situation had evolved, the presiding judge continued, one thing remained constant: Jews continued to be counted, listed, arrested, and deported.[46]

He pressed Papon: he wanted to know what the defendant made of the fact that invalids, the old, and the very old were being deported. It's the same question, he added, that could be asked about the children. What did you think? What did you imagine? Not extermination camps, Papon insisted.[47]

* * * * * * * * * * *

Addressing Papon during the fifty-seventh session, Michel Zaoui, the lead lawyer for the plaintiffs, pointed out that during pretrial hearings, Papon had declared that it was Jews who deported other Jews. Zaoui now asked: Do you really think Jews were responsible for their own deportation? No, of course not. But those were your very words. My comments applied only to Drancy—there Jewish detainees made up the final lists for deportation.[48] Blaming others constituted Papon's chief line of defense.

It was his superior, Maurice Sabatier, the regional prefect, Papon maintained, who was the responsible party. Every time Papon was asked about a document he had signed that dealt with arrests or internments, he uniformly replied: "By delegation." And that delegation of signature did not indicate a delegation of competence: he was no more than a "paper pusher" (a "porte-plume," literally a "pen-holder"), a mere factotum with no discretion whatsoever.[49]

Zaoui called him out, but in such a polite fashion that Papon was momentarily disarmed. He intended, the lawyer began, to pose some simple questions to understand better the relations between the two men, to understand better the climate in which the two of them had worked together. After all, they had known each other since 1935, and that long association had engendered mutual trust. It was Sabatier who had brought Papon to Bordeaux; he had requested that Papon come collaborate with him. And every day Papon reported to his chief. So the question Zaoui asked was this: Could the defendant describe an ordinary day, one without any particular problems? Could he enlighten the court on that?

Touched by Zaoui's courtesy, Papon gave the following account of a typical morning at the prefecture. He arrived between 8:00 and 8:30 and spent the next several hours sorting out papers; he made a preliminary triage, serious matters in one pile, purely administrative affairs in another. Then going through the first pile again, he did another triage, selecting those items requiring the attention of the prefect. Along the way, he signed various documents and met various people. Toward the end of the morning, he joined Sabatier in the prefect's office.[50]

Here Zaoui interrupted: You arrived in his office with the dossiers you wanted to talk over with him and when you left, a decision had been reached, a joint decision of the prefect and his secretary-general. Was there common agreement between you and Sabatier? I have found documents that demonstrate the "osmosis" between the two of you. Then turning to the jury, Zaoui continued, Sabatier and Papon worked in tandem for two years. Papon, after having consulted and discussed serious matters with his patron, then signed and gave orders for arrests.

Papon, realizing that he had fallen into the trap Zaoui had carefully set, tried to object: the osmosis was not systematic. You are making a generalization, and I protest.[51]

Zaoui would have none of that: I can show the osmosis that existed between you and Sabatier, I can show that when the prefect was absent, you substituted for him, that decisions were taken in common. Can you give an example of a disagreement between the two of you?

The presiding judge seconded Zaoui's request. At this point, Papon's memory, which up until now had been remarkable, failed him. Clearly, the tandem Sabatier-Papon handled Jewish questions, and those questions were never a source of conflict. Clearly, Papon facilitated the plan to get rid of the Jews, to despoil them, and to ship them toward a cruel fate.[52]

* * * * * * * * * * *

At the beginning of April 1998, the trial concluded. The jury was asked to respond to 764 questions. For each of the victims specifically named, the jurors had to decide whether he or she had been the subject of an illegal arrest, an arbitrary detention, or murder; then whether these actions amounted to persecution carried out on behalf of a state practicing a hegemonic political ideology. Finally was the accused guilty of having knowingly aided the preparation or consummation of the acts in question?[53]

After deliberating for nineteen hours, the jury rendered its verdict: conviction on some of the charges of illegal arrest and arbitrary detention, acquittal on all the charges of murder, on the grounds that Papon didn't know where the trains were going. The sentence: ten years imprisonment. To some, a disappointing outcome. Still the jury had made crystal clear: to deliver children to the secret police is as large a crime against humanity as one ever needed to find, no matter where they were going, or what kind of car they were going to travel in.[54]

That Papon was tried and condemned—even though he escaped conviction on the murder charge—Zaoui considered a battle won.[55] A French court had proved willing to pass judgment on a high official, and later a minister, for assisting the Nazis in deporting Jews. "Acting in accordance with administrative policy," the verdict announced and did so loudly, "does not relieve" civil servants "from having to answer personally for those actions."[56] "The men with stamps and filing cabinets now couldn't plead procedure any more than soldiers could plead orders."[57]

IV. Coda

In July 2012, at a commemoration to mark the seventieth anniversary of the Vél d'Hiv roundups, President François Hollande reaffirmed what Chirac had said seventeen years earlier. "The truth is hard, cruel. The truth is that French police arrested thousands of children and families. Not one German soldier was mobilized for this operation. The truth is this was a crime committed in France, by France."[58]

"For the French Republic," Hollande continued, "there cannot and will not be any lost memories." In the years between Chirac and Hollande's speeches, the polemics had quieted down, but, at the same time, school teachers had found it increasingly difficult to teach about the Holocaust. "The Shoah," Hollande insisted, "is not the history of the Jewish people, it is history, our history …. There must not be a single institution where this history is not fully understood, respected and pondered over."[59]

Along with this commitment to memory, Hollande also made a commitment to fighting anti-Semitism. "Anti-Semitism is not an opinion," he said, "it is vileness." And it must be faced directly. "It must be named and recognized for what it is. Wherever it manifests itself," it must be "unmasked."[60]

2

Germans in the Dock

At Nuremberg, the prosecution charged not just men, but so-called criminal organizations as well. This charge—one of the most controversial in the entire proceedings—was meant to make possible any number of subsequent prosecutions based on evidence of a person's membership in a group declared to be criminal.

In his opening statement for the prosecution, Robert Jackson laid out the political concerns that informed the indictment.

> It seems beyond controversy that to punish a few top leaders but leave this web of organized bodies unscotched in the midst of German post-war society, would be to foster the nucleus of a new Nazidom. The members ... still nourish a blind devotion to the suspended, but not abandoned, Nazi program .... If ... [these organizations] are exonerated here the German people will infer that they did no wrong and will easily be regimented in reconstituted organizations under new names, behind the same program.[1]

In the end, the tribunal declared only three organizations to be criminal: the SS, the Gestapo-SD, and the "Leadership Corps" of the Nazi party. And those who had knowledge of the organization's criminal purposes and who had joined voluntarily—with the outbreak of the war on September 1, 1939, as the starting date—would be held liable. At the same time, in conformity with the maxim that a person should be considered innocent until found guilty, the burden of proof regarding knowledge and the voluntary nature of membership fell to the prosecution.[2]

These organizations, Jackson claimed, "were not so extensive as to make it probable that innocent, passive, or indifferent Germans might be caught up in the same net as the guilty." Not every policeman, he noted, not the ordinary police, stood accused, and similarly the "average soldier or officer, no matter how high-ranking," was not blamed.[3] The full extent of complicity in the Final Solution may well have been beyond the ken of prosecutors in the years immediately following the war. That changed in the mid-1990s. The publication of Daniel Goldhagen's book, *Hitler's Willing Executioners,* and the *Vernichtungskrieg (War of Annihiliation)* Exhibition brought home to the postwar German public, as never before, the terrible reality of mass participation in the Holocaust.

I. Willing Executioners

How did uniformed police end up engaging in military or quasi-military operations? How was a civilian institution transformed into a fighting force— and an active participant in the extermination of Jews?

In the wake of Germany's defeat in the First World War, as revolution broke out, as the army dissolved, military officials organized counter-revolutionary paramilitary units known as the Freikorps. Once the domestic situation quieted down, many Freikorps members joined the regular police, ready at hand to quell any further revolutionary threats. During the 1920s, policemen, stationed in barracks, represented a barely disguised violation of the Versailles Treaty which limited the size of Germany's standing army. The Allies objected, but not very strenuously.[4]

In 1936, three years after assuming power, and a year after reintroducing conscription in open defiance of the Versailles Treaty, Hitler put Heinrich Himmler, Reichsführer-SS, in charge of both the political and uniformed police. Himmler, in turn, divided the German police forces into two branches: the first, the Security Police (Sicherheitspolizei) Main Office, under Reinhard Heydrich, was made up of the Secret State Police (Gestapo) and the Criminal Police (Kripo); the second, the Order Police (Ordungspolizei) Main Office, under Kurt Daluege, had charge of the city and municipal police (Schupo), the small-town police (Gemeindepolizei), and the rural police (Gendarmerie). Over the next several years, the Order Police expanded rapidly, and by 1939, it had grown to roughly a quarter of a million men.[5]

In June 1941, on the eve of the German invasion of the Soviet Union— codename Operation Barbarossa—Major Ernst Weis of Police Battalion 309 met with his company commanders. He informed them of two orders—which were to be passed on verbally to all units, army and police alike, moving into Russia. The first, the notorious Kommissarbefehl, or commissar order, directed that all so-called political commissars, that is, all Communist functionaries in both the Soviet army and civil administration, be executed. The second, the Barbarossa decree, took German actions against Russians out of the jurisdiction of military courts, thus making Russian civilians fair game. According to the historian Christopher Browning, "Major Weis then went further. The war, he said, was a war against Jews and Bolsheviks, and he wanted it understood that the battalion should proceed ruthlessly against Jews. In his view, the meaning of the Führer's order was that the Jews, regardless of age or sex, were to be destroyed."[6]

> After entering the city of Białystok, Major Weis on June 27 ordered his battalion to comb the Jewish quarter and seize male Jews, but he did not specify what was to be done with them. That was apparently left to the initiative of the company captains .... What started as a pogrom—... beating, humiliation, beard burning, and shooting at will—... quickly escalated into more systematic mass murder. Jews collected at the marketplace were taken to a park, lined up against a wall, and shot. The killing lasted until dark. At the synagogue, where at least 700 Jews had been collected, gasoline was poured on the entryways. A grenade was tossed into the building, igniting a fire. Police shot anyone trying to escape. The fire spread to nearby houses in which Jews were hiding, and they too were burned alive. The next day, thirty wagonloads of corpses were taken to a mass grave. An estimated 2,000 to 2,200 Jews had been killed.[7]

This is the bare outline. How to account for this murderous behavior was to become the subject of heated controversy.

* * * * * * * * * * *

The publication of *Hitler's Willing Executioners* in 1996 provided publicity for Browning's book, *Ordinary Men*, which had appeared four years earlier. Both featured Reserve Police Battalion 101.

During the first twenty months of the war, the battalion had made two forays into Poland. In September 1939, it accompanied a German army group to Kielce. There behind German lines, it rounded up Polish soldiers and patrolled a POW camp. At year's end, it returned to its Hamburg base and engaged in further training. In May 1940, it was sent to the Warthegau, one of the four regions of western Poland annexed to the Reich. This venture lasted a year. Initially in Posen, subsequently in Łódź, the battalion carried out "resettlement actions." (As part of Hitler and Himmler's demographic scheme to "Germanize" these newly acquired regions, that is, to populate them with "racially pure" Germans, all Poles and other so-called undesirables—Jews and Sinti and Roma—were to be expelled.)[8] Then between May 1941 and June of the following year, the battalion's chief—and most notorious—duty involved assisting in the deportation of Hamburg Jews. Four of the fifty-nine transports that, from mid-October 1941 to late February 1942, carried more than 53,000 Jews and 5,000 Sinti and Roma from the Third Reich "to the East" came from Hamburg.

Each time it was recalled to its native city, the battalion underwent considerable changes in personnel. In December 1939, about a hundred of its career policemen were transferred to create additional units and roughly the same number of middle-aged reservists took their places. In May 1941, all the remaining prewar recruits below the rank of noncommissioned officer were distributed to other formations, and once more the battalion was filled out with reservists. At this point it was a pure reserve battalion. By June 1942, when it was assigned another tour of duty in Poland, only a few of its noncommissioned officers had been on the first Polish action and less than 20 percent of the men had been on the second. Some had witnessed atrocities in Posen and Łódź. Others had learned something of the mass murder of Jews in Minsk and Riga. But for the most part, the battalion was "now composed of men without any experience of German occupation methods in eastern Europe," or for that matter—with the exception of the very oldest who were First World War veterans—any kind of military service.[9]

With a total strength of roughly 550 men, the battalion comprised a staff and three companies. Major Wilhelm Trapp, aged fifty-three, served as senior officer. After the First World War, in which he had distinguished himself and received the Iron Cross First Class, he became a career policeman and rose through the ranks. In 1932, he joined the Nazi Party and thus technically qualified as an "Old Party Fighter." But he was never taken into the SS, and his young captains came to regard him as weak and unmilitary. The two of them were in their twenties and also held the equivalent SS rank of Hauptsturmführer. A lieutenant commanded the third company: close in age to Trapp, and like him, he was merely a party member.

How Nazified was the battalion? Reserve police battalions were much less so than their regular counterparts. "Of the 550 men, 179 were Party members, composing 32.5 percent of the battalion …. Seventeen of the Party members were also in the SS." Being a party member was a "rather ordinary distinction"; far more significant is the fact that only 3.8 percent of the men were in the SS, "the association of true believers." As a group, "the men of Police Battalion 101 were not an unusually Nazified lot for German society."[10] On the face of it—and here Browning and Goldhagen were in agreement—"these men would not seem to have been a very promising group from which to recruit mass murderers on behalf of the Nazi vision of a racial utopia 'free of Jews.'"[11]

* * * * * * * * * *

On June 20, 1942, the battalion headed east once again: it entrained at the same station from which some of its men had deported Hamburg's Jews. Several days later it arrived in the Lublin District of German-occupied Poland. There Himmler's crony, the "brutal and unsavory Odilo Globocnik," directed the murder of Jews, principally, though not exclusively, in extermination camps.[12] By chance, when the battalion reached the scene, the camps, due to technical difficulties, had suspended operations. Globocnik grew impatient and decided to use firing squads for mass executions. And so Reserve Police Battalion 101 found itself with orders to slaughter Jews in Poland.

Browning gave pride of place to the first such slaughter—the rounding up and murdering of 1,800 Jews in Józefów. On the morning of July 12, just as the sun was rising, Trapp addressed his men. He explained the battalion's assignment: to ship male Jews of working age to labor camps; to shoot women, children, and the elderly. Then he made an extraordinary proposal: "any of the older men who did not feel up to the task before them could step out." Trapp was unequivocal—those who came forward were excused from the operation. Ten or twelve men got out of line. As the day progressed and the reality of what was required sank in, the number of men asking for a different task grew. Direct requests—when funneled up to Trapp—were granted. Some policemen sought other ways to evade the killing: idling about, slowing down, or temporarily absenting themselves. Trapp himself managed to stay away. He spent most of the time "either in a schoolroom converted into his headquarters, at the homes of the Polish mayor and the local priest, [or] at the marketplace."[13] He did not witness the executions.

Once the roundup was completed, the men of First Company proceeded to systematic murder. (As the Jews were being chased to the assembly area, there had been plenty of killing—the sick and elderly, and maybe even infants.) They were taught how to fire a fatal shot, one meant to bring death instantaneously. An initial contingent then went to a forest several kilometers from Józefów. When a truckload of Jews arrived, an equal number of policemen came forward and were paired with their victims. Together they marched down a forest path, where the victims were ordered to lie down in a row. "The policemen stepped up behind them, placed their bayonets on the backbone above the shoulder blades ... and fired in unison." In the meantime, more policemen had appeared at the edge of the forest and filled out a second firing squad. The next batch of Jews was taken further into the forest and, again, ordered to lie down and shot. Except for a midday break, the shooting procedure went on without interruption until nightfall.

But the pace proved too slow. If the task were to be finished in a single day, more units needed to be pressed into service as executioners. So Trapp ordered Second Company to join the killers in the forest. In contrast to First Company, these men received no information on how best to proceed. They had difficulty firing properly; they shot freehand, missing or wounding their victims; then they tried aiming point blank at the back of the neck—with gruesome results, blood, bone splinter, and brains spraying everywhere. The forest was so full of dead bodies that it was difficult to find places for the remaining Jews to lie down. And no plans were made for burial; the corpses were just left lying in the woods. At roughly 9:00 p.m.—seventeen hours after Reserve Police Battalion 101 had first arrived at the outskirts of Józefów—darkness fell and so did the last Jews marked out for slaughter.

Five weeks later, Second Company received orders to murder the Jews of Łomazy. Set for August 17, this was a joint operation with a unit of Hiwis—"volunteers" (Hilfwilligen or Hiwis) recruited from Ukrainian, Lithuanian, and Latvian POWs and usually assigned the most grisly tasks. Of the crimes committed by the battalion, Goldhagen gave most space to this massacre. Where Browning claimed that sadism was not a common feature,[14] Goldhagen argued otherwise: the cruelties began early and ended late.

It started with the roundup: "The Jews were no longer unsuspecting.... They attempted to hide and thus ... escape annihilation. Everywhere in the Jewish quarter there was shooting .... After 2 hours or so ... the Jewish quarter was cleared." Herded together, the Jews lingered for hours, without food or drink. Then the trek to the execution site got underway. When the slaughter was at last ready to start—after another pause, this time with the victims in a state of undress and lying prostate under the hot sun—fifteen to twenty Jews at a time were compelled to run a gauntlet with the Germans shouting at them and beating them with rifle butts. The killing site itself was something out of hell:

> The pit ... was between 1.6 and 2 yards deep, and about 30 yards wide by 5.5 yards long. It sloped down at one end. The Jews were forced to clamber down the incline and lay themselves face down. [In the meantime, the Hiwis had appeared.] ... [S]tanding in the pit and using rifles, [the Hiwis] put a bullet in the back of each Jew's head. The next wave of Jews had to lay themselves down on top of their bloodied and skull-bursted predecessors. Using this method the pit gradually filled up. The Hiwis, who ... [drank] steadily, aimed ... badly, even at close range .... As if this were not gruesome enough, the pit had been dug below the water table. The rising water mixed with blood and the bodies floated about.[15]

Eventually the Hiwis became too drunk to carry on. So the Germans were pressed into service: to avoid contact with the floating corpses, they positioned themselves on opposite sides of the pit's earth wall and proceeded to fire on the Jews. They kept at it for a couple of hours, by which time the Hiwis had sobered up and could finish the job.

And then there were the photographs Goldhagen reproduced: some taken on the day of the massacre, several showing the assembled Jews waiting to be marched off for execution, one showing them digging the mass grave. He merely described others, including a snapshot of a detachment posing "right before their final departure from Łomazy, days after the … slaughter. The Germans' … obvious good cheer displayed for the camera, was their own contemporary final commentary on the time they passed in this town, its defining feature having been their transformation of a half-Jewish town into a *judenrein* one."[16]

And the battalion continued to massacre Jews. In staggering numbers: 38,000 shot to death and another 45,000 shoved into trains bound for Treblinka. For a battalion of approximately 550 men, "the ultimate body count was at least 83,000 Jews."[17]

* * * * * * * * * * *

At a conference held at UCLA in the spring of 1990, Browning had talked about the sources he was exploiting for his research project on Battalion 101 and had conjectured that different "historians reading the same set of … [documents] would not produce or agree upon an identical set of 'facts' beyond an elementary minimum."[18] He proved prescient. At a symposium sponsored by the Holocaust Memorial Museum in Washington, D.C., six years later, he confessed that he had not imagined that "a confirming example of an alternative history would be forthcoming so quickly or so starkly."[19]

What were the documents in dispute? In 1960, the Zentrale Stelle der Landesjustizverwaltungen (Central Agency for the State Administrations of Justice) in Ludwigsburg, West Germany had begun an investigation into the battalion. Once it was convinced that the case should be pursued, it turned the matter over to the prosecutor's office in Hamburg. The Hamburg bureau identified, located, and interrogated 210 former members of the battalion. Many were interrogated more than once. Fourteen men were indicted, and their trial began in October 1967. After a lengthy appeal process, the sentences of only three were upheld. This outcome may seem inadequate; yet "most investigations of police battalions did not even lead to indictments," let alone convictions.

As Browning put it, "Comparatively speaking the investigation and trial of Reserve Police Battalion 101 was a rare success for German judicial authorities attempting to deal with the police battalions." And almost everything historians know about the battalion's role in the murder of Polish Jews "is based on the testimony contained in … these interrogations."[20]

In reviewing Browning's work, Goldhagen found fault with the methodology, with Browning's too ready acceptance of protestations of innocence.

> Anyone who has worked with these materials … will agree that the overwhelming tendency of the perpetrators is to distance themselves from the deeds. Plausibly, or implausibly, they often assert that they were not present at the mass killings. If that can be proved false, then they admit to having been present, yet maintain that they did not pull the trigger but carried out other duties. And if that claim, too, cannot withstand scrutiny, then they own up to having pulled the trigger, but only under duress.

As a result of his credulity, Goldhagen claimed, Browning overestimated the number of men in the battalion who did not become killers. Browning's figure of roughly 20 percent, Goldhagen considered too high and "not supported by the evidence."[21]

Goldhagen found fault with Browning's interpretation as well. When it came to pressures the murderers experienced as coming from their peers, Browning imagined how the men thought and felt. "Since the battalion had to shoot even if individuals did not," he wrote, "refusing to shoot constituted refusing one's share of an unpleasant collective obligation. It was, in effect, an asocial act vis-à-vis one's comrades. Those who did not shoot," he continued, "risked isolation, rejection, and ostracism—a very uncomfortable prospect within … a … unit stationed among a hostile population."[22] But in sharp contrast, Browning shied away from exploring the perpetrators' ideological commitments. Goldhagen objected:

> In line with his entire approach, Browning does not seriously investigate two central issues: What did these men think of Jews? And what were their attitudes toward mass murder as a "solution" to the so-called "Jewish Problem"? … Browning assumes, without articulating it clearly, that these men, upon receiving orders to kill Jews regarded these orders as immoral. He seems to believe that what needs to be explained is the manner in which they were conditioned by their immediate social circumstances to become killers in spite of their principled disapproval.

Those circumstances, Goldhagen maintained, "cannot account for the Germans' behavior."[23]

What could? Goldhagen's answer was German, not Nazi, anti-Semitism. German society, he claimed, was unlike any other: it was thoroughly anti-Semitic. Jews were regarded as a clear and present danger that could only be met by elimination.

> The eliminationist mind-set that characterized virtually all who spoke on the "Jewish Problem" from the end of the eighteenth century onward was … [a] constant in Germans' thinking about Jews. For Germany to be properly ordered, regulated, and, for many, safeguarded, Jewishness had to be *eliminated* from German society …. "The German *Volk*," asserted one anti-Semite … ,"needs only to topple the Jews' in order to become united and free."[24]

Goldhagen continued: "What 'elimination'—in the sense of successfully ridding Germany of Jewishness—[actually] meant, and the manner in which this was to be done was unclear and hazy to many." Yet even in the late nineteenth century, German anti-Semitism was "pregnant with murder."[25]

How did German anti-Semitism ripen into a program of extermination? Goldhagen did not tackle this question. He made no claim to providing a detailed historical account. In short order, he moved from the late nineteenth century to 1933 and even then paid scant attention to the period 1933 to 1939. Instead he offered an "aerial overview" and from that height, he discerned an equivalence between German and Nazi anti-Semitism. "Whatever else the Germans thought about Hitler and the Nazi movement," he insisted, "however much they might have detested aspects of Nazism, the vast majority of them subscribed to the underlying Nazi model of Jews."[26]

In preparing the assault on the Soviet Union, Goldhagen argued, Hitler finally made the move to extermination. (Goldhagen acknowledged, albeit in an endnote, that, among historians, there is enormous controversy over how and when Hitler decided on the Final Solution.)[27] Once Operation Barbarossa was underway, it became clear to the Germans involved, "officers and enlisted men alike, that the eliminationist ideology was finally to be implemented in its most uncompromising … form." Both the leadership and those executing the plans "pursued the Jews' destruction with a single-mindedness that, as a rule, shunted other objectives aside …. Annihilating European Jewry became, [along] with the war and at times even of higher priority than the war, the central mission of the German juggernaut."[28]

Browning had entitled his book *Ordinary Men*. "The policemen in the battalion who carried out the massacres," he wrote, "like the much smaller number who refused or evaded, were human beings. I must recognize that in the same situation,

I could have been either a killer or an evader—both were human."[29] Goldhagen would have none of that. The subtitle of his volume read *Ordinary Germans*. "The men of Reserve Police Battalion 101," he argued, "were not ordinary 'men,' but ordinary members of an extraordinary political culture, the culture of Nazi Germany, which was possessed of a hallucinatory, lethal view of the Jews. That view was the mainspring of what was, in essence, voluntary barbarism."[30]

* * * * * * * * * *

In early 1996, months before a translation of Goldhagen's book appeared, German critics pounced. The highbrow liberal weekly *Die Zeit* ran a front-page editorial asking, "Were All Germans Guilty?"[31] The answer was yes, if Goldhagen were to be believed. In eight subsequent issues, *Die Zeit* devoted page after page to reviews of the book by leading historians and political scientists. Other papers followed suit. The message of this early commentary could be summed up as "Don't Read This Book."[32]

Distinguished scholars panned the work as unoriginal, sensationalist, and worthless. Norbert Frei insisted that "the historical empirical yield" of the book was meager, that a big chunk was based on "secondary literature," that it offered "few novelties" for those who were well informed.[33] Eberhard Jäckel chimed in: Goldhagen's book was "riddled with errors"; it represented a "relapse into the most primitive of stereotypes"; it was "simply bad."[34] Hans Mommsen, dean of German Holocaust studies, did not beat about the bush either: the book "falls behind the current state of research, rests on insufficient foundations and provides no new insights."[35] Reviewing the reviews, Hans-Ulrich Wehler concluded: many dismiss the book, ostensibly on the grounds of expert knowledge, but perhaps they do so "in the service of a latent defense mechanism which aims to keep the horrors of our past at a safe distance."[36]

Such was the situation in late August when Siedler Verlag brought out the German translation. The title, *Hitlers Willige Vollstrecker*, *Hitler's Willing Executors*, is slightly softer that the original "Executioners." Otherwise it was practically identical to the English edition. The conventional wisdom that Siedler had missed its chance by publishing the book more than three months after the uproar in the German press proved mistaken. Without any publicity whatsoever, the first printing immediately sold out; within the next few weeks more than 130,000 copies had been shipped to bookstores. And when Goldhagen himself appeared on the scene in September, sales sky-rocketed, sending the book to the top of the bestseller lists.

Goldhagen's promotion tour to multiple cities turned into a "triumphal procession," as *Die Zeit* called it.[37] Tickets at 15 DM ($10) were snatched up, creating a thriving black market. In Hamburg, 700 people found seats or standing room in the Kammerspiele theatre; some 300 more waited outside. "Those who could not get into the Frankfurt Opera House for Goldhagen's debate with his critics nearly demolished the foyer. In Berlin, a thousand people gained access by waiting in long queues; another thousand waited in vain. In Munich, the organizers were able to change the venue at the last moment to the Philharmonic, where all 2,000 seats were filled."[38] Wherever Goldhagen went, he was followed by a train of reporters and cameramen, begging for yet another interview, coaxing him to take part in yet another talk show. For ten days, it was virtually impossible to open a newspaper or turn on the TV without confronting a flattering image of the boyish Harvard political scientist.

It was in Berlin that a highly contentious encounter with Mommsen took place. The German historian determined to set the young American straight. His condescending and school-masterish manner—he was a man in his late sixties—irritated the audience, and there were boos when he spoke. At one point he claimed that many of the killers had not been clear in their own minds about their motives. Goldhagen quickly turned the situation to his advantage: "'Is there anyone in this room,' he asked, 'who agrees with Professor Mommsen that the people who murdered the Jews didn't know what they were doing?'"[39] In a trembling voice, his face red with anger, "Mommsen protested that he had been misunderstood, that he had intended to say only that there was more than a single cause for what they did. It was too late."[40]

In Berlin, and Munich as well, the moderator wondered at Goldhagen's popularity. He asked the panelists why so many people had bought the book and were now sitting here. They evaded the question. Commentators offered an answer: "The public clearly preferred Goldhagen's ... [clear-cut] argument to Mommsen's convolutions, statements like, 'The structure of the regime, based on the permanent competition of disintegrating institutions, together with a negative selection in the perception of political interests, drove forward a process of cumulative radicalization in a direction, at the end of which was, inevitably, the destruction of the Jews.'"[41] In contrast, Goldhagen had a simple message: the executioners were only too "willing," and they included not only rigorously chosen SS monsters but also the fathers and grandfathers of today's Germans. Volker Ullrich, writing in *Die Zeit*, put it this way: "Here is finally someone who expressed what has for so long been taboo: that the distinction between 'criminal

Nazis' and 'normal Germans' is false; that the readiness to murder millions of Jews came from the middle of German society."[42]

Then the descriptions—the detailed accounts of cruelties committed against Jews by "ordinary Germans." Goldhagen forces the reader to see the hand on the trigger or holding a whip, to witness the pleasure the perpetrators took in killing and torturing. To "bring the abstract horror of a million-fold annihilation down to flesh and blood," and thereby produce an emotional reaction: so it was with Goldhagen's book.[43]

And the moralizing tone of the work. Browning's *Ordinary Men* has no explicitly moral voice, and its implicit message that practically anybody could have taken part in the killing in Poland, "leaves the moral puzzle untouched." Goldhagen interrupts his account with questions such as: "How could any person have looked upon these pitiable sick Jewish women without feeling sympathy for them, without feeling horror at the abject physical condition in which they had been plunged?" Culpability, "carefully circumscribed for decades, ... was all of a sudden spread lavishly throughout yesterday's Germany."[44]

In January 1997, the *Journal for German and International Politics* awarded Goldhagen its Democracy Prize.[45] And it seemed richly deserved. He may have made exaggerated claims and overlooked important causes other than a particular brand of anti-Semitism. But by focusing attention on the moral issue, he stirred the conscience of a newly unified Germany.

II. Crimes of the Wehrmacht

Goldhagen estimated that, all told, the number of hands-on perpetrators reached 100,000.[46] The Wehrmacht, a conscript army, counted some 18 million. "The Holocaust may not have been a 'national project,' as Goldhagen ... [claimed], but the war definitely was." The assertion that it was "a criminal undertaking that facilitated the genocide of the Jews meant that millions of soldiers who had served in the ranks of the Wehrmacht could not escape blame."[47] No wonder, then, that the Wehrmacht exhibition caused even greater discomfort than the publication of *Hitler's Willing Executioners*.

Created almost as soon as the war ended, the myth of a clean Wehrmacht took hold in the early 1950s. At Nuremberg, Wehrmacht generals stated, under oath, that:

> (a) the relationship between the army and Hitler had always been cool and distant; (b) they had rejected the pre-war persecution of the Jews as unworthy of

the German people, and during the war they had neither control nor knowledge of it; (c) ... [they] had accepted the war against the Soviet Union as a preventive war forced on the German people ... ; and (d) they had waged the war according to the rules of international law; the partisan war had been initiated by Stalin,... and the German response had been both necessary as a protective measure and carried out as a military operation.[48]

In short, they portrayed the German army as a professional organization that had little in common with Hitler's worldview and had fought a host of enemies with remarkable tenacity and skill.

For political reasons, both domestic and international, the depiction of German soldiers as just doing their jobs was readily accepted. It seemed impossible to rebuild West German society without a narrow definition—as narrow as possible—of so-called Nazis and their accomplices. "The idea that the Wehrmacht as such might be a criminal organization ... would have implicated such vast portions of German society ... that one would have had either to declare a general amnesty (thereby legitimizing the notion of unpunished crimes) or to give up altogether the ... [idea] of resurrecting some form of German national unity."[49] Neither of these options was realistic particularly in the context of the Cold War. Not only was it unthinkable to eliminate Germany as a nation, but it quickly came to pass that the hopes of some Nazi leaders and Wehrmacht generals were realized, namely, that Germany would be a crucial factor in a Western anti-Communist alliance.

* * * * * * * * * * *

Vernichtungskrieg: Verbrechen der Wehrmacht 1941 bis 1944 (*War of Annihilation: Crimes of the Wehrmacht, 1941–1944*) grew out of a project on "Civilization and Barbarism" launched by the Hamburg Institute for Social Research. Its purpose was to investigate the destructiveness of the twentieth century on the eve of the new millennium. "The war conducted by the German state between 1939 and 1945 was an obvious subject of research, especially the campaign against the Soviet Union: this constituted a new type of unlimited warfare, in which the moral law was annulled and criminality became the norm."[50]

The exhibition covered the period 1941 to 1944. It was limited to a few sectors of the front and presented its evidence through three case studies: the extermination of Jews and the massacre of other civilians in occupied Serbia in 1941; "the role of the Sixth Army in assisting SS-Einsatzgruppen in the mass murder of Jews during the invasion of the Ukraine in the summer and autumn of 1941, and in subjecting the rest of the civilian population to ruthless terror"; and the destruction of Jews, prisoners of war, and other civilians in occupied Byelorussia. The documentation for the show came "mainly from the Freiburg Military Archive (part of the German Federal Archive), along with additional materials from German and Soviet trials, and collections of letters and diaries. Apart from a few official propaganda photographs, all the photographs in the exhibition were taken by German soldiers, and were confiscated when they fell into the hands of the Red army or Tito's partisan units."[51] The scene at a cemetery wall in Pančevo—an officer is pointing a pistol at a Serbian hostage— was reproduced repeatedly, including on the cover of *Der Spiegel*,[52] and quickly became the visual icon of the crimes committed by the Wehrmacht.

The exhibition initially met with approval. The major German daily and weekly newspapers greeted it as a remarkable contribution to the fiftieth anniversary of the war's end.[53] "The most important historical exhibition for many years and certainly the most troubling," wrote Karl-Heinz Janssen in *Die Zeit*. "The terrible truth," he continued, "has been revealed ... a truth that had previously been unable to prevail against a wall of consensual public silence in Germany."

And visitors came in large numbers. Between 1995 and 1999, the exhibition traveled to thirty-four cities in Germany and Austria and was seen by an estimated 850,000 attendees. The co-sponsors in the cities where it was shown were "the institutional pillars of liberal public opinion," and it was accompanied by a series of events meant to continue discussion and reinforce its message. In "Stuttgart and Erfurt, the exhibition took place in the trade-union headquarters, in Regensburg in the premises of the Protestant Education Bureau. In Nürnberg, the list of co-hosts included the city archives, the local history workshop and the regional section of the International Physicians for the Prevention of Nuclear War; the five weeks of the exhibition were punctuated by talks and panel discussions involving representatives of the *Bundeswehr*, academic historians, writers ... as well as films and guided tours of the site of Nazi party rallies."[54] Even the Minister of Defense seemed ready to concede that as "an organization of the Third Reich, the Wehrmacht was involved in the crimes of National Socialism through its leadership, military units, and individual soldiers. That is why, as an organization, it cannot serve as a foundation for any tradition."[55]

In several cities, the exhibition provoked public debate, but that debate remained on a local or regional level. The 1997 opening in Munich marked a turning point. In the traditionally conservative Bavarian capital, the exhibition became the object of serious political dissension, with far-right and leftist groups organizing rival demonstrations. Roughly 5,000 supporters of the extreme right—mainly skinheads dressed in bomber jackets and heavy boots—marched through the center of the city, giving the Hitler salute and singing Nazi songs. Bearing aloft black, red, and white banners of the neo-Nazi National Democratic Party, the procession headed for the plaza opposite the town hall where the exhibition was being shown. A counter-demonstration of approximately 8,000 left-wingers tried to block the extremists, "some hurling eggs, bricks, and bottles at the neo-Nazis."[56] Elsewhere in the country, police arrested young extremists en route to Munich; in Berlin they seized a man carrying two mines and detonators; near Halle, they stopped a busload of Nazi supporters after explosives, detonators, knives, iron bars, and baseball bats were found on board.

The neo-Nazi demonstration was, if not encouraged, then at least countenanced by the Christian Social Union, the sister party of Helmut Kohl's Christian Democrats. Leading circles of the CSU heaped abuse on the exhibitions. Peter Gauweiler, chair of the Munich CSU, attacked head-on the exhibition's creators: he challenged Jan Philipp Reemtsma, heir to a tobacco fortune, to devote his wealth, not to "the memory of murdered Jews, captured Red army soldiers and civilians suspected of being partisans," but to the victims of cigarette smoking; he claimed that Hannes Heer, as an active communist and as someone convicted of committing serious bodily harm—both charges were untrue—was in no position to judge the Wehrmacht.[57] In addition, he sent a letter to over 300,000 Munich households urging people to shun the exhibition. This advice was echoed by the Bavarian education minister: he recommended that schools stay away. Despite these pleas, 90,000 visitors, including 20,000 school children, turned up.[58]

* * * * * * * * * * *

In March 1997, the Bundestag was still housed in Bonn—it moved to Berlin two years later. Members of a leftist party—the Party of Democratic Socialism (PDS)—proposed that the exhibition be shown in the foyer. The speaker turned the scheme down. In the wake of this back and forth, the Bundestag held an extraordinary plenary session—to debate the pros and cons of an exhibition produced by a private research institute.

It quickly became a forum for personal memories. Members started to talk about their family histories, and suddenly the human face of the war was present in the chamber. For example, Otto Shily (Social Democratic Party—SPD):

My uncle Fritz, a man of sterling character, was a lieutenant in the Luftwaffe ....
At the end of the war, ... in despair over the crimes of the Nazi regime, he sought

death in a hail of bullets from a low-flying enemy aircraft. My oldest brother, Peter Shily, refused to join the Hitler Youth and tried to flee Germany. When that failed, he volunteered for the front. After a brief training, he was assigned to fight in Russia, suffered serious wounds, lost an eye and the movement of an arm. My father, an extraordinary entrepreneurial personality, … was a declared opponent of the Nazi regime. Nevertheless, as a reserve officer who had served in the First World War, he felt humiliated when he was not called up for military service because of his membership in the Anthroposophical Society, a society that the Nazi had banned. Only later did he realize the insanity—I'm using his own words—of that standpoint. My wife's father, Jindrich Chajmovic, an unusually courageous and self-sacrificing man, fought as a Jewish partisan in Russia against the German Wehrmacht. Now I am going to say something, which, in its severity and clarity, must be accepted by me and by all of us: the only person whom I have named here—the only one—who risked his life for a just cause was Jindrich Chajmovic.[59]

And Christa Nickels (Green Party):

My father was not young when he went to war. He was born in 1908 and died in 1991. He was not a party member …. Later he was drafted. My mother told me that in the 1950s my father … screamed terribly in his sleep about fire and children. She said it was simply horrible. Naturally, I loved my father very much …. Several years ago … I noticed for the first time that my father, in the only photo of him that we have from that time, is wearing a uniform that is black and that has skulls on it …. I was already a representative of the Greens in the Bundestag and didn't dare ask my father; it was incredibly difficult for me …. Fifty years after the attack on Poland, … our Green Alliance caucus … [was] in Majdanek …. [O]ne night I simply broke down because I was terribly shocked by what happened in Majdanek, but just as much by what they did to men, one of whom was my father. They were for the most part men who loved life and children. It was horrible what they made out of men in this criminal war. Most of them didn't have the strength to extricate themselves from it. All of them made themselves guilty of infinite atrocious wrongs. The men, women, and children—I am the daughter of such a German soldier—we are still marked by that today.[60]

In the sometimes tearful atmosphere of personal revelation, the various proposals for and against the exhibition were touched on only lightly. A few days later, politics returned to their usual state. The Christian Democrats proved unwilling to show the exhibition in the Bundestag foyer: it was not their job, they claimed, to judge or evaluate private initiatives. The following month, they pushed through a motion rejecting any "generalized condemnation of members of the Wehrmacht."⁶¹

* * * * * * * * * * * *

Two years later, in 1999, several young scholars unleashed a torrent of criticism that led to the closing of the exhibition. Two stood out, both of them from Eastern Europe with right-wing sympathies. The Polish historian Bodgan Musial claimed that some of the photographs did not depict victims of the Wehrmacht; rather they showed bodies of men and women executed by the NKVD (the Soviet secret police). The Hungarian historian Krisztián Ungváry asserted that in some of the snapshots he recognized Hungarian and Finnish, but no German, uniforms. Accusations came thick and fast: some photos showed one and the same event under different captions; in a number of cases the order of photographs was changed, and as a result of being reshuffled, they assumed a different sense; in some captions the servicemen's titles were wrongly stated; several quotations were arbitrarily redacted and so on.⁶²

In the face of this public scandal, the directorate of the Institute and the exhibition board decided to close the show. It had been scheduled to open in New York in December.⁶³ That too was called off. Shortly thereafter, Reemstma appointed an independent commission—of which Omer Bartov was a prominent member—to evaluate the historical validity of the photographic and documentary evidence. Precisely one year after the exhibition closed, the commission submitted its findings.

The report noted that a few photographs had been mislabeled, twenty out of 1,433, and did not belong in the show, and that some of the explanatory statements were too sweeping. At the same time, the commission "rejected all charges of falsification and manipulation."⁶⁴ It made crystal clear:

> The basic assertions of the exhibition regarding the Wehrmacht and the war of extermination in the "East" remain ... correct. It is incontrovertible that in the Soviet Union the Wehrmacht not only became "entangled" in the genocide perpetrated on the Jews, in the crimes against the Soviet prisoners of war and in the war against the civilian population, but that it participated in these crimes partly in a leading and partly in a supporting capacity. Hence this is not a matter of isolated "infringements" or "excesses," but of actions emanating from decisions made by the highest military authorities and by the troop commanders at the front and behind the front.⁶⁵

In November 2001, a second exhibition with a modified title, "Crimes of the Wehrmacht: Dimensions of a War of Annihilation 1941 to 1944," opened in Berlin.

* * * * * * * * * * *

The introduction to the new exhibition begins with the statement: "The war against the Soviet Union differed from all other European wars of the modern era, including campaigns waged by the Wehrmacht against other countries during the Second World War."[66] Laws of war served as a framing device, and this legalistic perspective meant that the central claims of the original Wehrmacht exhibition appeared in a different light. It suggested that the Holocaust in occupied regions could be explained on the basis of a "law-free zone" created by "criminal orders." How to account for the persecution and deportation of Jews by Wehrmacht units in parts of occupied Europe where the international laws of war were adhered to—in France, for example? What about the racist aims and objectives of the Nazis? Certainly a great number of German soldiers murdered Jews and Commissars not simply because they were ordered to, but because they hated Jews and Jewish Bolsheviks.[67]

Instead of holding fast to the argument that the troops, as well as their commanders, were responsible for genocidal crimes, the new exhibition shifted the spotlight to the leadership of the Wehrmacht. It focused on how the generals made genocide possible, from forcing Jews to wear yellow stars to giving orders for murder. One could now see a photocopy of the injunction, dated October 10, 1941, issued by the commander of the Sixth Army, Field Marshall Walter von Reichenau, demanding that soldiers "show understanding for the necessity of a just retaliation against Jewish sub-humans"—and how quickly these sentiments were echoed in decrees circulated by Field Marshall Gerd von Rundstedt and General Erich von Manstein.[68] This time, as *Der Spiegel* observed, "it was no longer soldiers, but Hitler's generals in the dock."[69]

As for the number of soldiers who took part in war crimes, the spokeswoman for the show explained: "It is not possible to say anything about that. Any figure ... apart from zero would be entirely speculative."[70] The directors of the new exhibition sought to avoid generalizations about the behavior of the troops. The soldiers were not a homogeneous mass; they were individuals, who, in making decisions, had choices. The part of the exhibition labeled "Scope for Action" illustrated this claim. In October 1941, three company commanders of the 691st Infantry Regiment received one and the same verbal order: to eliminate all the

Jews in their occupation zone. "First Lieutenant Hermann Kuhls executed it immediately; Captain Friedrich Nöll demanded written confirmation and only then executed it; First Lieutenant Josef Sibille refused to execute it. Having been asked by the battalion commander: 'When will you show firmness at last?' Sibille answered: 'Never.' *And he was in no way punished for that.*"[71]

The main emphasis now moved from photographs to texts. Instead of a collection of striking photographs—provoking questions about the possible involvement of one's parents or grandparents—the revised exhibition presented a chain of texts. In an area of 1,000 square meters, orders, reports, and communiqés documenting the criminal activity of the Wehrmacht appeared in temporal and thematic sequence. A visitor might suppose that he or she was entering a study area, so overwhelming was the abundance of source material and supporting literature. A "history clinic" was how one commentator characterized it. "White boards bear long texts and white chairs" invited visitors to spend time with the evidence.[72] The new exhibition did not shock, and it did not aim to.

And it was well received. Between its opening in late 2001 and its permanent move to the Deutsches Historisches Museum in 2004, more than 400,000 people viewed it. What was central to all the media coverage was the difference between the two exhibitions. "The emotional disturbance triggered by the Wehrmacht Exhibition" was still in critics' minds, and the second version was judged against that background. The German press underlined the exhibition's "sobriety," its "scholarliness," its "strict objectivity." Writing in the *Frankfurter Allgemeine Zeitung*, Michael Jeismann praised the new exhibition as a "good piece of consensus history."[73] The exhibition's spokeswoman concurred: "For the moment, that is a very good way of putting it."[74]

By the time of the second exhibition, the legitimacy of the claim that the Wehrmacht took part in the planning and execution of an unprecedented war of annihilation was rarely called into question. Denial of war crimes, including involvement in the Holocaust, had now become a revisionist position.

III. Coda

In early 2013, the German public tuned into a television miniseries *Unsere Mütter, unsere Väter* (translated into English, strangely enough, as *Generation War*). Sensationally popular in Germany, with something like 7 million viewers—decidedly less so in Poland where its depiction of anti-Nazi partisans as unkempt anti-Semites provoked outrage—the series portrays an enormous range of experience: vicious combat with the Red Army, ambushes, life in a wartime hospital, moments of shock and disillusionment. All by way of what happens to five friends who are presented as more or less typical young Germans.

At the beginning of the series, three men and two women, all roughly twenty years old, dance and drink in a Berlin bar. The time is June 1941. Two of the men, brothers, are heading for the Eastern Front. Wilhelm, stern and responsible, squares his jaw and does his duty. His bookish younger brother, Friedhelm, "serves in the same unit, but hates war and mutters bitter asides between battles." The brothers are fond of Greta, "a singer who wants to be the next Marlene Dietrich, and her lover, Viktor, a Jewish tailor" who has managed (how?) to get by in Berlin. "The fifth member of the group is Charlotte, called Charly … an ardent and idealistic nurse …. Except for Viktor, they all do terrible things." The brothers take part in executions; Charly betrays a Jewish colleague at the earliest opportunity; Greta sleeps with a loathsome SS officer, first to protect Viktor, then to boost her career. The series acknowledges what scholars have established that "the Wehrmacht played a major role in committing atrocities in occupied countries."[75]

Still, the historian Ulrich Herbert wrote, the miniseries fails. The story begins just at the moment when enthusiasm for Hitler and for National Socialism reached its high point. Here one sees none of it, nothing of the trust and love Hitler aroused, nothing of the conviction that Europe should be ruled by Germany—and that it would be better if Jews were to disappear.

> Our fathers and mothers were not just young people, who simply wanted to live, but could not because of the war, as the miniseries suggests …. [They belonged to] a highly ideological, politicized generation that wanted German victory, wanted the victory of National Socialist Germany, because they thought it was right.[76]

3

Victims, Jewish and German

In 1992, two years after German reunification, Chancellor Helmut Kohl declared his intention to turn the Neue Wache (New Guardhouse) into his country's national memorial to the "victims of war and tyranny." This formula equated soldiers fighting for Hitler with Jews herded into gas chambers. There were protests. Nevertheless, Kohl pushed ahead.

Built between 1816 and 1818, the Neue Wache was the first major commission given to the celebrated Prussian architect Karl Friedrich Schinkel. For a century this model of restrained German neoclassicism served the soldiers assigned to guard the king. The end of the monarchy in 1918 robbed it of its original purpose. The Weimar Republic gave it a new one: to memorialize those killed during the First World War. To that end, Heinrich Tessenow was entrusted with the task of revamping the interior. His work found favor with the Nazis: they kept the memorial largely unchanged and used it as a backdrop for their official day of mourning. Near the close of the Second World War, the Neue Wache was heavily damaged in an air raid.[1]

During the 1950s, the German Democratic Republic reconstructed the building, rededicating it in 1960 to the victims of fascism and militarism. At the end of the decade, the interior was redesigned: stones embedded in the floor marked the graves of an Unknown Soldier and an Unknown Resistance Fighter; urns containing earth from Second World War battlefields and concentration camps were set in the floor as well. The message conveyed was one of brotherhood between German soldiers slain in battle and anti-fascist fighters incarcerated in concentration camps. Jews were not mentioned.

Even before reunification, Kohl's way of honoring victims had provoked a furor. In 1985, he had persuaded President Ronald Reagan to accompany him to a German military cemetery in the town of Bitburg.[2] The graves he asked Reagan to honor were of soldiers who fought against the United States in the Second World War. Unfortunately, Bitburg also turned out to be the resting place of forty-nine Waffen-SS troops. From this point on, the ritual unraveled. Kohl felt that for the American president to back out of the visit would amount to a public disavowal. The president's advisers thought that either sloppy staff work or bad faith on the part of the Germans had placed Reagan in an embarrassing position. In response to American pressure, the day's itinerary was expanded to include a visit to the Bergen-Belsen concentration camp memorial site. With a re-fashioned Neue Wache, there would be no more Bitburgs; there would be a place where foreign dignitaries could lay wreaths on appropriate occasions.

Kohl personally approved not only the restoration of Tessenow's design, but also the major deviation from it: placing at the heart of the memorial a massive enlargement of Käthe Kollwitz's "Mother with her Dead Son," a sculpture resembling a Christian Pièta. Kollwitz's work, inspired by the loss of her child at the front in the First World War, represents God's mercy and pity for all—for all German soldiers, with no explicit distinction between the Wehrmacht and the SS—and also for those involved in war crimes and crimes against humanity. Were Jewish Holocaust victims presumed to figure among those memorialized? If so, critics argued, this Christian symbol was highly unsuitable.

The chairman of the Central Council of Jews in Germany, Ignatz Bubis, objected. In an effort to appease him, and to guarantee his attendance at the opening ceremony scheduled for November 14, 1993, a bronze plaque with an inscription making an unequivocal reference to Jewish victims was added to the façade. Kohl's staff chose a passage from an address given by Richard von Weizsäcker, the Federal Republic's president, to the Bundestag on the fortieth anniversary of Nazi Germany's defeat. In Weizsäcker's speech, the victims of the Germans, headed by the Jews, were singled out and the Germans themselves mentioned only afterwards. In the revised and edited version, all the dead and suffering were mixed together before enumerating Nazi victims. The intent of the president's declaration was entirely distorted. It is safe to say that Bubis had been misled.[3]

Within a decade of the Neue Wache rededication, plans to build a major Berlin memorial specifically devoted to Jews slaughtered in the Holocaust were finalized. Here was a clear expression of a commitment "to honor the murdered victims ... and to admonish all future generations never again to violate human rights."[4] At just about the same time, the publication of Jörg Friedrich's *Der Brand* (*The Fire*), following upon W. G. Sebald's *Luftkrieg und Literatur* (*The Air War and Literature*), focused attention on the Allied bombing campaign that had devastated German cities.[5] This fresh preoccupation with German suffering—like the rededication of the Neue Wache—came at the expense of Holocaust memory.

I. Creating a Memorial

On October 11, 1998, Martin Walser, one of Germany's most prominent postwar writers, upon receiving the prestigious Peace Prize of the German Book Trade, gave a speech from the pulpit of the historic Paulskirche in Frankfurt. The speech, to an audience of approximately 1,200 political and intellectual dignitaries, turned out to be anything but peaceful.

"Everybody," he said, "knows the burden of our history."

> No serious person denies Auschwitz; no person who is still of sound mind quibbles about the horror of Auschwitz; but when this past is held up to me every day in the media, I notice that something in me rebels .... I begin to look away .... I try to seek out the motives of those holding up our disgrace, and I am also happy when I believe I can discover that often the motive is no longer keeping alive the memory, or the impermissibility of forgetting, but rather the exploiting of our disgrace for present purposes ....

> Now I tremble with my own audacity when I say: Auschwitz is not suited to become a routine threat, a means of intimidation or moral bludgeon that can be employed on any occasion, or even a compulsory exercise .... But what suspicion does one invite when one says that the Germans today are a perfectly normal people, a perfectly normal society?[6]

When Walser finished, the audience gave him a standing ovation. "Only Bubis and his wife remained sitting, stony-faced, refusing to applaud." A day later, he accused Walser of "intellectual arson"—an accusation he later retracted.[7]

Holocaust remembrance, so Walser implied, amounted to a new kind of tyranny. Here he singled out the proposed Memorial to Murdered Jews in Berlin: "a nightmare the size of a football field" in the center of the restored German capital. It would be the "monumentalization of our disgrace."[8]

* * * * * * * * * * *

The Berlin memorial was the brainchild of Lea Rosh, a prominent television journalist. Accompanied by the historian Eberhard Jäckel, she had visited Yad Vashem in 1988 to film a documentary about the Nazi murder of European Jews. "Something like this," she thought, "should exist in the country of the perpetrators, a memorial, a site of remembrance, something that recalls THIS DEED."[9]

Why only the Jews? The insistence that their murder alone should be memorialized struck many as preposterous. What of the 500,000 Sinti and

Roma, the 3.2 million Soviet prisoners of war, as well as homosexuals and members of various political and religious groups? If racist victimization was the criterion, then certainly the Sinti and Roma should be included; and so too the homosexuals and the euthanasia victims—the first to be gassed—because their deaths were all connected to aspects of racial ideology. In the course of the 1990s, the federal government made commitments to honor each victim group—and these commitments took a good deal of the heat out of the debate.

Where should the memorial be located? This, too, was initially a source of controversy. The demolition of the wall freed up a large tract of land, in the middle of a suddenly unified Berlin, from the Potsdamer Platz to the Brandenburg Gate. The site that in 1992 was designated for the memorial lay on the northern part of old ministerial gardens. It was in fact neither where Hitler's chancellery once stood—the place Rosh preferred—nor where his bunker had been situated (both of which were already slated for federal states' offices). Berlin's building director assured critics that the neutral location did not mean that the city was trying to suppress memories of Nazi terror; rather those memories would now be centralized at a convenient spot.[10]

* * * * * * * * * * *

How could an artist's design give form to Germany's need to remember the Holocaust? A first attempt was a notable failure.

Throughout the early 1990s, Rosh and the citizens' group she had organized pressed forward. Together with the federal government and the Berlin city authorities, they sponsored a competition for the future memorial. Twelve internationally recognized artists were invited to submit proposals. There were another 516 entrants. The competition's guidelines advised participants that they had five acres at their disposal. Most of them were determined to use all of it.

The designs ran the gamut from the beautiful to the grotesque, from the high modern to the low kitsch, from the architectural to the conceptual. One artist proposed an immense Ferris wheel equipped not with compartments for thrill-seekers but with sixteen freight cars like the ones in which Jews were transported to death camps. Another envisioned a sixty-foot high oven modeled on those used to cremate murdered Jews, which would burn round-the-clock.[11] Someone else "called for creating a container 130 feet tall and 100 feet wide as a symbolic vessel for the blood of six million." Then there was the proposal for "a series of bus stops whose coaches would take visitors to the sites of actual destruction throughout Berlin, Germany, and Europe."[12] And there were numerous variations on gardens of stones, broken hearts, and rent Stars of David.

The winning entry "consisted of a gargantuan, twenty-three foot thick concrete gravestone, in the shape of a three-hundred foot square, tilted at an angle running from six feet high at one end to twenty-five feet high at the other. It was to be engraved with the recoverable names of 4.5 million Jews, and in the Jewish tradition of leaving small stones at a gravesite to mark a mourner's visit, it was to have some eighteen boulders from Masada ... scattered over its surface .... Eighteen is the Hebrew number representing *chai* or life, so the number of stones seemed right."[13] That they should be brought from Masada seemed altogether wrong. (According to the Jewish historian Josephus, at the end of the Jewish revolt against the Romans, 66–73 C.E., zealots held out at Masada, their last stronghold. And to prevent the Romans from enslaving them, they committed suicide. Would bringing stones from Masada suggest a troubling equation between suicide and murder? Would it imply that the Jews of the Holocaust had brought on their destruction themselves?)

The design drew immediate criticism. Bubis hated it; so too did Kohl, who rescinded the government's support for the winner of the competition. "Germany's 'Memorial for the Murdered Jews of Europe' seemed to have been sunk by its own monumental weight—and once again Germany was left pondering its memorial options."[14]

At the same time dozens of articles and op-ed pieces appeared in the daily press. "An entire volume was produced in a matter of weeks comprising the objections of some three dozen critics, artists, and intellectuals." Emblazoned on the back cover were the words of James E. Young, an American professor of English and Judaic Studies. "If the aim is to remember for perpetuity that this great nation once murdered six million human beings solely for having been Jews, then this monument must remain uncompleted and unbuilt, an unfinishable memorial process."[15] Young was to play a leading role in selecting the winner in a second competition.

* * * * * * * * * * *

In January, March, and April 1997, the memorial's organizers called for a series of public colloquia. Young, who had written extensively on traditional monuments, was among the artists, historians, and curators invited to suggest how the process of deciding upon a memorial design could get moving again.[16] When, during the third colloquium, it came his turn to speak, he abandoned his carefully prepared text. He admitted that up to this point, he had been a skeptic—and that, indeed, he had been "making a fine career out of skepticism."

> Rather than looking for a centralized monument, I was perfectly satisfied with the national memorial debate itself. Better, I had thought, to take all those millions of Deutsch marks and use them to preserve the great variety of Holocaust memorials already dotting the German landscape: ... from the excellent learning center at the Wannsee Conference House to the enlightened exhibitions at the Topography of Terror at the former Gestapo headquarters, both in Berlin; from the brooding and ever-evolving memorial landscape at Buchenwald to the meticulously groomed grounds and fine museum at Dachau; from the hundreds of memorial tablets marking the sites of deportation to the dozens of now-empty sites of former synagogues—and all the spaces for contemplation in between.

But, he added, he had become uneasy: "Our unimpeachable skeptical approach to the certainty of monuments was now beginning ... to look like so much hand-wringing and fence-sitting, even an entertaining kind of spectator sport."[17]

The day after his intervention, Young was asked by the Speaker of the Berlin Senate to join a Finding Commission of five whose task was to choose a suitable memorial design. The other four were the directors of the Deutsches Historisches Museum in Berlin and the Kunstmuseum in Bonn, as well as one of Germany's preeminent twentieth-century art historians and one of Berlin's most widely respected and experienced architects. They "would be given free rein" to extend the process as they saw fit and "to make an authoritative recommendation to the Chancellor and the memorial's organizers."[18] Young was the only expert on Holocaust memorials; he was the only foreigner; and he was the only Jew. Because of his religion, one fellow juror acknowledged, Young "had an entirely different legitimacy."[19]

How to proceed? Initially the committee "hammered out a list of twenty-five artists and architects who would be invited to submit a sketch and a conceptual abstract." Nearly all of them, "including some of the most radically skeptical," agreed to participate. Over the course of three days, the commission "held private, two-hour seminars in front of each design board, reading aloud the designers' rationale, weighing ... the liabilities and promise of each proposal." The commission then selected what they regarded as the eight strongest and asked the artists to present their work in person. The jurors unanimously agreed that two, one by Gesine Weinmiller, a young German architect, and the other by Peter Eisenman and Richard Serra, well-known Americans, an architect and a sculptor, stood out for their balance of "brilliant concept and powerful execution."[20]

It so happened that Kohl strongly favored the Eisenman-Serra design—with some caveats. He invited the team to explain it to him in person. As an artist, Serra was adamant in refusing to make any changes whatsoever: he viewed the stipulations as undermining "the work's internal logic and integrity." Consequently he withdrew from the project, implying that once altered, it "would in effect no longer be the work of art he had proposed." Eisenman, as "an architect who saw accommodation to his clients' wishes as part of his job," agreed to modify the design.[21] His revised model found favor with Young and his colleagues, and in a report, written by Young, all five enthusiastically recommended it to Kohl, the Berlin authorities, and the citizens' group.

* * * * * * * * * * *

Eisenman's design had nothing in common with conventional memorials. It is an abstract plan of 2,711 concrete stelae set across the space. The ground, uneven and undulating, sways beneath the stelae so that each one is some degrees off vertical. Arranged in a precise rectilinear array, fifty-four rows running from north to south, eighty-seven rows running from east to west, with long, straight, and narrow alleys between them, they are identical in their horizontal dimensions, but differ in height varying from eight inches to more than fifteen feet tall. The concrete of the stelae, neutral in tone and smooth in texture, could be impregnated with an anti-graffiti solution to make them easy to clean. Ironically, swastikas, yellow stars of David, and other drawings painted on the stelae, would have defined the site more clearly as a Holocaust memorial.

Eisenman rejected all signs indicating the name, dedication, or purpose of the memorial. The Finding Commission appreciated his wish that the stelae "remain under-determined and open to many readings." In their abstract form, they could "accommodate the references projected onto them by visitors …. This is not a bad thing." Still—the jurors suggested that "a permanent, written historical text be inscribed on a large tablet or tablets set into the ground or onto the ground, tilted at a readable angle."

> This position will bring visitors into respectful, even prayerful repose as they read the text, with heads slightly bowed in memory. These could be placed at the entrance or on the sides, under the trees lining the perimeter of the field, leaving the integrity of the field itself formally intact …. Thus placed, the memorial texts will not create a sense of beginning or end of the memorial field, leaving the site open to the multiple paths visitors take in their memorial quest.[22]

When the memorial was finally built, Eisenman prevailed: there was no written text.

* * * * * * * * * *

By the time the Finding Commission made its recommendation, national elections were looming, with Kohl's Christian Democrats behind in the polls. Near the end of the campaign, Michael Naumann, culture-minister designate of Gerhard Schröder's Social Democrats, was asked whether or not an SPD government would back going ahead with Eisenman's Holocaust memorial. No, he answered, and with that the memorial became an electoral issue dividing Kohl and Schröder and their two parties. After handily defeating Kohl, Schröder entered into a so-called red-green coalition with Joshka Fischer's Green Party. "Because the Greens supported the memorial, the coalition agreement stipulated that the memorial be put to a vote in the Bundestag."[23] Before that was taken in June 1999, Naumann lobbied—successfully—for an interpretive center, something approaching a national museum, to share Eisenman's field of waving stelae. How big? How would it fit into the site?

In the end, the Information Center was located underground. It is not immediately visible to the passer-by and many visitors are unaware of its existence. A Berlin photographer's experience is not unusual: "I can't find the special emotion related to the real Holocaust in this concrete field .... You could think it's just a place for children to play hide-and-seek." Having seen the Information Center, he felt differently: "if you initially go to the museum and then view the memorial, it is very moving."[24]

The exhibition begins with a chronology of the Holocaust, starting in 1933. Then four rooms follow, each of which fulfills a different function: to display excerpts from personal accounts written by Jewish men and women of the verge of annihilation; to present an overview of Jewish family life—and fates—in occupied Europe; to repeat aloud the names, along with short biographies, of thousands of victims; and to map and describe, with words and photographs, sites of persecution and extermination. Finally, an information portal offers a repository of victims' names from Yad Vashem and supplies a database of Holocaust museums and memorials throughout the world.[25]

Where the field of stelae is abstract, the Information Center is concrete; where the former is impersonal, the latter is personal from start to finish. The foyer sets the tone. Six photographs with the subject looking directly at the camera greet the visitor, six lives, six deaths: Robert Vermes, born 1924 in Slovakia, arrested March 27, 1942, deported and murdered at Majdanek; Malka Malach, Polish, mother of seven, perished in Auschwitz in 1943; Etty Hillersum, born 1914, lived in Amsterdam, deported, along with her family, from the Westerbork transit camp to Auschwitz on September 7, 1943; Zdeněk Koňas, age eleven, deported from Prague to Theresienstadt on July 8, 1943, and from there to Auschwitz on September 6, 1943; Simon Mandel, a fifty-seven-year-old tradesman, deported in 1944 from Northern Transylvania, then part of Hungary, to Auschwitz; and Claire Brodzki, born in Lyon in 1928, deported to Auschwitz in late May 1944, died on June 20, 1945, a few months after the liberation of the camp.

The Information Center is deceptively powerful. The light is dim; replicas of letters, photographs, and other testimonies of truncated lives are soberly shown. The gravity of the voices that recite the names and short biographies of Holocaust victims create a solemn sonic experience. The effect on visitors is immediately perceptible: they pause in silence; their discomfort is visible. In an unexpected reversal, it is the Information Center, rather than the field of stelae, that has become the site of Holocaust remembrance.[26]

* * * * * * * * * * *

The removal of more than 1,400 stelae out of the 4,200 originally projected opened up the space and made room for tourist buses to discharge their passengers. And visitors arrived in droves: since the inauguration of the memorial in May 2005—seventeen years after it was first proposed—millions of people have come to see the field of stelae and the Information Center. They quickly joined the ranks of sights "not to be missed."

The Vietnam Memorial in Washington, D.C., to which the Berlin memorial is sometimes compared, commemorates Americans, not the Vietnamese whom American soldiers slaughtered. In contrast, the Germans gave up five acres in the middle of their capital city to a memorial to those who were murdered, murdered in their name. This was unprecedented. "The objective of the Memorial," Eisenman wrote, "was to touch not only the Jewish survivor families, but most importantly, the Germans."[27]

Was Walser correct? "Germans today," he insisted, "are a perfectly normal people, a perfectly normal society." Would the memorial stand as a "moral bludgeon," a "monumentalization" of German disgrace?[28] The philosopher Jürgen Habermas took a different line.[29] Germans ought to embrace the Holocaust, he argued, as an "element of a broken identity."[30] In a letter to Eisenman, he wrote, "the monument should be a sign that the memory of the Holocaust remains a constitutive feature of the ethical-political self-understanding of the citizens of the Federal Republic."[31]

II. German Suffering Revisited

Running parallel with debates over what form a Holocaust memorial should take were calls for Germans to remember the suffering they had endured under Allied, principally British, bombs.

> [T]he strategic bombing surveys published by the Allies, together with the records of the Federal German Statistics Office and other official sources, show that the Royal Air Force alone dropped a million tons of bombs on enemy territory; ... that of the 131 towns and cities attacked, some only once and some repeatedly, many were almost entirely flattened, that some 600,000 German civilians fell victim to the air raids, and that three and a half million homes were destroyed, while at the end of the war seven and a half million people were left homeless, and there were 31.1 cubic meters of rubble for every person in Cologne and 42.8 cubic meters for every inhabitant of Dresden.[32]

This was Sebald speaking. Friedrich repeated what he said, at much greater length and to much greater acclaim.

The British enthusiasm for bombing was a creature of the emergency facing them in the summer and autumn of 1940. After the evacuation from Dunkirk in late May and early June, it was necessary to show the public that military action against Germany had not been abandoned. Churchill hoped—rather desperately—that bombing Germany would—as RAF leaders repeatedly asserted—"compel Hitler to abandon invasion plans or even ... dislocate the German war effort."[33] The sorties carried out in the summer of 1940, however, produced negligible results. And they invited retaliation.

The sustained German night attacks—relying as they did on the preponderant use of incendiaries as opposed to high-explosive bombs—showed the British what a serious bombing offensive looked like. In late September 1940, the Research and Experiments Department of the Ministry of Home Security supplied a detailed study of the effects of German bombs on different types of targets—oil storage, gas works, power stations, aircraft production. "It is axiomatic," ran the report, "that fire will always be the optimum agent for the complete destruction of buildings, factories etc." The department recommended using high-explosive bombs to create the "essential draught conditions" in damaged buildings, followed by heavy incendiary loads, and completed with more high explosives to hamper the enemy emergency services.[34]

The shift to "area bombing" is usually associated with Air Marshal Sir Arthur Harris who took over as Commander-in-Chief of Bomber Command in February 1942. Just days before his arrival, officers in the Air Ministry had put in place the strategy they preferred: incendiary attacks on industrial areas. They had issued a directive removing communications as a primary target and focusing instead on "the morale of the enemy civil population and in particular of industrial workers."[35] Through death or absenteeism, it was expected that factory output would be seriously reduced. Harris, an aggressive and single-minded defender of Bomber Command's mission, was determined to demonstrate what his forces could do.

In March and April 1942, he ordered concentrated incendiary attacks on Lübeck and Rostock. Their centers were medieval, densely packed, and inflammable. In May, he put together 1,041 aircraft to strike Cologne. More than 5 percent of the city's buildings were damaged or destroyed. But it had proved impossible to wipe out the city, as Harris had hoped. A little more than a year later, he saw hopes of that sort realized.

The series of raids against Hamburg, appropriately named "Operation Gomorrah," were spread over ten days from July 24–25 to August 2–3, 1943. On the first night 728 British bombers hit targets in and around the city. The next day 218 American aircraft aimed at the submarine yards, and fifty-four flew in on the following day. The RAF raid on the night of July 27 stands as a textbook example of the previous two years' planning. Summertime conditions—high temperatures and low humidity—helped. The aircraft concentrated their 2,326 tons—1,200 of which were incendiaries—on crowded working-class districts. Numerous fires joined up to produce a roaring inferno, which, in turn, "created a pillar of hot air and debris that rose quickly to a height of more than two miles above the city. Greedy for more oxygen, the fire drew in cold air from the surrounding area with such force that the new winds reached hurricane ... strength ... , collapsing buildings, uprooting trees and sucking human bodies into the flames .... Acting like giant bellows, the winds ... [generated] temperatures in excess of 800C ... [and] destroyed everything combustible barring brick and stone .... An area of more than 12 square miles was burnt out."[36]

Harris was not yet finished. Intent on destroying the city, he ordered two more raids, July 29–30 and August 2–3. Though large residential areas were again torched, neither resulted in a second thermal hurricane. Smoke made it impossible for British airmen to assess the effects. Local police authorities did the counting, later revised: 61 percent of Hamburg's houses and apartments were damaged or destroyed; 900,000 inhabitants evacuated the city; 37,000 people died. This last figure represents the single largest loss of civilian life in one city in the course of the whole European war, exceeded only by the 100,000 Japanese killed in the fire-bombing of Tokyo and the atomic attacks on Hiroshima and Nagasaki.[37]

But it is Dresden that has been singled out as an example of excessive and unjustified destruction. The aiming point was the historic city center, which, in the event, was entirely blackened. The assault on February 13-14, 1945, was carried out in two successive waves, with 796 aircraft, carrying 2,646 tons of bombs, including 1,181 tons of incendiaries. The first wave was not very effective; the second, with the bulk of the forces, flying in clear conditions, "achieved an exceptional level of concentration." Low humidity and dry weather, plus a large number of small fires, proved ideal conditions for causing another firestorm. The flames consumed fifteen square miles of the city. "Out of 220,000 homes, 75,000 were destroyed. The firestorm, like the Hamburg conflagration, left bodies mummified or reduced to ash, making the final count difficult."[38] The best available estimate of those killed is 25,000. The attack on Dresden was undertaken in full knowledge that the city was filled with civilian refugees and hence likely to produce a very high number of casualties.

No other raid met with as much criticism. Within days, the American press was full of news that the Allies had adopted a policy of terror bombing. Army brass attempted to reassure the public that Dresden had been a legitimate military target, that it had been a key transport hub through which supplies of men and materiel were being delivered by rail to the Eastern Front. But it was hard to stifle the debate, either then or later.

In the end, how did the bombing campaign help bring about Germany's defeat? Once it became necessary to divert manpower and equipment for defense, the air war distorted German strategy, preventing military leaders from using airpower effectively at the front as they had done from 1939 to 1941. The fact that German fighter aircraft, guns, ammunition, and radar equipment were tied up in the Reich contributed to failure in Russia, in the Mediterranean theatre, and against the Allied invasion of France. "Without bombing, the German war effort would have been as free to optimize the use of resources ... as was the United States .... [But] this does not mean that civilians were *ipso facto* legitimate targets."[39]

After the war, Dresden was on the Soviet side of the "Iron Curtain," and, thus, from 1949 onward, in the German Democratic Republic. With the onset of the Cold War, Soviet and East German authorities seized on the bombing of Dresden as a propaganda weapon against Britain and the United States. Yet East Germany was not alone in recalling air raids. Cities in the Federal Republic also erected monuments to those killed and conducted official ceremonies to mark anniversaries of the aerial attacks. "The local press devoted whole pages to first-person stories, essays, and poetry, as well as to photographs of the destruction."[40] And national news outlets chimed in, dedicating special programs to the ceremonies or featuring accounts of them. Bombing losses, in Dresden and elsewhere, were far from forgotten.

The claim, then, that Sebald and Friedrich grappled with a topic previously off-limits—German suffering—was much exaggerated. So why this talk of a prohibition? It pointed to resentment of the reigning left-liberal focus on German crimes—a resentment that Walser articulated.[41] To put it simply: the Jews had been given their due; now it was time to consider anew the fate of the German civilian population.

* * * * * * * * * *

Starting in the 1960s, Sebald noted, writers in the Federal Republic reclaimed Auschwitz as their "own history." Eager to "compensate for the huge moral deficit ... which had been a feature of the postwar period," they denounced the "refusal to broach that monstrous subject." They denounced the earlier indifference and "collective amnesia." The experiences of Holocaust survivors were "no longer taboo in public discourse."[42] The experiences of Germans who have lived through the destruction of their cities, Sebald insisted, still were.

His *On the Natural History of Destruction* appeared posthumously. Sebald died in a car crash in 2001 at the age of fifty-seven. The book, lightly peppered with his trademark grainy photographs, consists of a long essay on the postwar reaction, or lack of it, to the Allied bombing campaign and three shorter articles on the German-language authors Alfred Andersch, Jean Améry, and Peter Weiss. The German edition, based on lectures delivered in 1997 and published two years later, included only two essays, the one on the bombing and the one on Andersch; a translator's note to the English version does not make clear who decided to add the Améry and Weiss pieces, but they are perfectly appropriate to the main essay.

Born in 1944, in a village in the Allgäu Alps, Sebald was too young and too geographically isolated to have memories of the war. Still, he felt that the horrors he had not experienced "had cast a shadow" over him from which he could "never entirely emerge."

> I had grown up with the feeling that something was being kept from me: at home, at school, and by the German writers whose books I read hoping to glean more information about the monstrous events in the background of my own life.[43]

There was, Sebald claimed, "a tacit agreement, equally binding on everyone, that the true state of material and moral ruin in which the country found itself" was to be ignored.[44] An example:

> People walked "down the street and past the dreadful ruins," wrote Alfred Döblin in 1945, after returning from his American exile … , "as if nothing had happened, and … the town had always looked like that."[45]

Another from a year later:

> Stig Dagerman, reporting from Germany … for [a] Swedish newspaper … , writes from Hamburg that on a train going at a normal speed it took a quarter of an hour to travel through the lunar landscape between Hasselbrook and Landwehr, and in all that vast wilderness, perhaps the most horrifying expanse of ruins in the whole of Europe, he did not see a single living soul. The train, writes Dagerman, was crammed full like all trains in Germany, but no one looked out of the windows, and he was identified as a foreigner *because* he looked out.[46]

Sebald continued: "The darkest aspects of the final act of destruction … remained under a kind of taboo like a shameful family secret, a secret that perhaps could not even be privately acknowledged."[47]

After reports about his lectures appeared in newspapers, Sebald received a number of letters "showing traces of uneasiness and distress still emerging in the minds" of their authors.

> A letter written in haste, … pours out fragmented memories of nights spent in the bunkers and underground railway tunnels in Berlin, images frozen in time, the disconnected comments of people talking about the jewelry they must save, or the salted beans lying in a tub at home, a woman with her hands closed convulsively on the Bible in her lap, an old man clutching a bedside lamp that for some unfathomable reason he had brought down with him. The letter, barely legible in places, emphasizes the clutching and clinging with double exclamation marks, speaking of "my trembling, my fears, my rage—still here in my head."

Obviously, this letter writer, and many others as well, found it painful "to go back over … traumatic experiences." Hence their "persistent avoidance of the subject, or aversion to it."[48]

If Sebald was distressed by the evasion of the public at large, he was angered by what he took to be the "self-imposed silence" of German writers. With the exception of Hans Erich Nossack, whose harrowing eyewitness account of the firebombing of Hamburg was published in Germany in 1948 as *Der Untergang* (*The End: Hamburg 1943*), they were unable or unwilling to tackle the topic of Allied bombing.[49] And German historians, Sebald claimed, were no better. "Known to be among the most industrious in the world," they have not yet "produced a comprehensive ... study of the subject." Only "Jörg Friedrich, in chapter 8 of his *Das Gesetz des Krieges* (*The Law of War*)," had taken a close look "at the evolution and consequences of Allied strategy .... Characteristically, ... his remarks ... [had] not aroused anything like the interest" they deserved.[50]

All that changed in the autumn of 2002 with the publication of *Der Brand* (*The Fire*).

* * * * * * * * * * * *

Born in 1944, the same year as Sebald, Friedrich has usually been described as an independent scholar. As a student, a Trotskyist and very much a man of 1968, he spent his early career writing about Nazi atrocities. That began to shift in the 1990s. The book Sebald singled out for praise, *Das Gesetz des Krieges*, "was a revisionist attempt to argue that the Wehrmacht's criminal war of extermination, especially on Soviet territory and against the Jewish people, was not in fact the product of racist and anti-Semitic doctrine, but the result of total war and the need to deter local populations ... [from] rebellion."[51] Then, in *The Fire* he set out to examine what he claimed had been a forbidden subject: the suffering of German civilians at the hands of the Western Allies, especially the British.

If Friedrich cannot be accused of nostalgia for the Third Reich, he did little to distance himself from those who could be. He chose the right-wing, mass-market tabloid *Bild-Zeitung*, Europe's largest circulation newspaper, to serialize parts of his book. The first installment "was laid out so that on either side of the headline were half portraits of Hitler and Churchill, both fixing their gazes at some point in space. The caption under Hitler read: 'The dictator started the mass bombing war.' Under Churchill was the statement that the British prime minister 'responded with many bombings.'"[52] It was as though Friedrich deliberately aimed his message at the crudest readership—not necessarily neo-Nazi, but relatively ill-informed, mostly illiberal, and prone to sensationalism.[53] By early 2003, the book had climbed to the top of German bestseller lists. And later that year, Friedrich published another bestseller, *Brandstätten* (*Sites of Fire*), even more sensational, with terrible images and scant commentary.[54]

What *The Fire* lacked—and it was much criticized for this deficiency—was historical context.[55] Using impassioned, yet opaque, rhetoric, he created the impression that British strategy had only one true objective: the total destruction of Germany, its cities and its people. The "annihilation principle" governed, and the British "did not ask ... questions."

> Terror does not seek to achieve anything .... Its success might be unconditional subjection, but even that does not end the horror. It makes no deals; its resolve is inscrutable and its aim, absurd .... It is subject to no rules: it is the rule. Everything that can be destroyed knows it is a target. That suffices.[56]

If the British calculated that the "annihilation zone" created on the ground would destroy Germans' morale, they made a mistake.

> Immediately after the war, the U.S. occupation forces extensively investigated the psyches of the bombing victims. They found that defeatism grew after the shock of the first attack experience. However, the accumulation of experiences tended to dull the effect. The soul did not rebel; it shriveled. Apathy and depression predominated. People felt an overwhelming need for sleep and none at all to overthrow Hitler.

And by keeping "hardship under control," with welfare measures of all sorts, including parceling out "property stolen from Jews who were then exterminated," the Nazis "cemented the bonds between people and regime as never before."[57]

Did people die as innocents or as soldiers? "Goebbels referred to the dead as 'fallen' who had given their lives in the field. They were buried with military honors staged by the party, with a drum roll as musical accompaniment." As late as February 1944, Hitler still "prohibited mass graves for the burial of bombing victims." His prohibition aimed to secure individual burial places for the "German national comrades as some final personal protection. It ultimately failed."[58] There were too many dead. In Dresden, ditches were dug at cemeteries to bury the thousands who had perished. Then mild weather accelerated the decomposition process, leaving the authorities with no choice but to incinerate the corpses.

> They were cremated at the Old Market, where iron girders were built into high grates on which roughly five hundred bodies ... could be stacked into a funeral pyre, drenched with gasoline and burned. These funeral pyres at the Old Market in Dresden represent a blemish in the history of our century that we will be hard

put to find another example of in the future. Whoever witnessed it will never forget that horrible scene as long as they live."[59]

Made up of Ukrainians, Latvians, and Lithuanians, who had served as guards in extermination camps, the units assigned to the task had learned their cremation procedures in Treblinka. The pyres continued burning for five weeks.[60]

Friedrich's narrative is filled with a sense of grievance. *The Fire* tells the same story over and over again of the extinction of a centuries-old urban environment. "At some point," Friedrich noted, "all the cities in the country had been destroyed by war once. But only once did war destroy all the cities."[61] Moving from north, to west, to south, and going on to Dresden and Berlin, he examined, city-by-city, the ruin of German towns. In *Brandstätten*, the choice, and especially the editing, of the pictures captures his lament for the ancient churches, medieval streets, baroque town halls, and rococo palaces that were obliterated. The first thirty-seven pages of the book are given to Germany, as it was, before the bombing campaign. In the end, he suggested that the loss of all this historic beauty was the real calamity.

In his catalogue of blows to German culture, Friedrich failed to include the "murder and expulsion of many of the best and most intelligent people of an entire generation."[62] He failed to mention the loss to Germany of the educated German-Jewish bourgeoisie.

* * * * * * * * * * *

What is *der Brand* (literally "fire" or "blaze") if not another word for holocaust? In suggesting that the British, and Americans, tried to flatten Germany's architectural treasures, Friedrich implied that they aimed to wipe out all traces of Germany's national heritage just as the Nazis sought to erase from Europe not only the Jews themselves, but their cultural legacy as well. In consistently using the German word *Vernichtung* (annihilation), he called to mind the *Vernichtungskrieg* (war of annihilation) conducted by the Germans in Eastern Europe. That is not all. Throughout, Friedrich echoed the idiom of the Holocaust: Bomber Squadron #5 became an "an elite task force"; cellars in which people took refuge and where they suffocated from lack of oxygen became "crematoria"; a firestorm became "mass extermination."[63]

What has often been said about the Holocaust, that is marked a rupture in civilization, Friedrich insisted was true of the strategic air offensive.[64] Could both murdered Jews and German bombing victims be remembered and mourned—without claiming moral equivalency?

III. Coda

In early 1986, Andreas Hillgruber, a well-known and well-respected diplomatic historian published a slim volume, *Zweierlei Untergang: Die Zerschlagung des Deutschen Reiches und das Ende des europäischen Judentums* (*Two Sorts of Collapse: The Destruction of the German Reich and the End of European Jewry*). Though politically conservative, he was no apologist for Nazism; nor had he ever sought to seal off Hitler from the rest of German history. The major essay in this little book focused on the defense of Germany's East Prussian front in the winter of 1944–5. What is striking was Hillgruber's demand that the reader "identify himself with the concrete fate of the German population in the East and with the desperate and sacrificial exertions of the German army of the East and the German fleet in the Baltic, which sought to defend the population from the orgy of revenge of the Red Army, the mass rapes, the arbitrary killing, and the compulsory deportations."[65] As a pendant to the larger piece, Hillgruber included a short essay on the annihilation of the Jews. Their suffering was not evoked: "no sealed freight cars, purposeful starvation, flogging, degradation, and final herding to the 'showers.' … If indeed these two experiences are two sorts of destruction, one is presented, so to speak, in technicolor, the other in black, gray, and white."[66]

Roughly a decade and half later, Günter Grass, a Nobel Prize winner and, at the time, considered Germany's greatest living writer, published *Krebsgang* (*Crabwalk*).[67] In his novella—which quickly became a bestseller—Grass, like Hillgruber, fastened on German suffering. He told the story of the torpedoing of the German ship *Wilhelm Gustloff* by a Soviet submarine on January 30, 1945, the twelfth anniversary of the Nazis' coming to power. He also told the story of how the ship came to be built, how the Nazis commissioned it in 1937 as part of the "Kraft durch Freude" ("Strength through Joy") program, and how they named it in honor of a Nazi party official who had been shot to death in Switzerland. "The *Gustloff* transported the right sort of Germans—those who met the criteria for inclusion in the racial state—to far-off places, offering chances for relaxation and foreign travel to those who had never enjoyed such pleasures."[68] In 1945, the ship, leaving the Baltic coast from a port near Danzig, was carrying refugees fleeing from the oncoming Red Army. Also on board were nearly 4,000 submarine recruits, some soldiers, 370 naval personnel, and anti-aircraft guns. As many as 9,000 passengers drowned.

Hauled out of the sea by a German rescue team, the narrator's mother, Tulla, gave birth to him, Paul. Despite his mother's constant urging, he has no interest in the circumstances of his birth. But, idly browsing the internet, he comes across a website devoted to keeping Gustloff's memory alive. Slowly he begins to realize that the "clever young fanatic" behind it is none other than his son, Konrad, a high school student whom he rarely sees and who now lives with Tulla.[69]

Konrad, prompted by Tulla, has become obsessed with the Gustloff affair. For his history class, he wrote a paper on the "Kraft durch Freude" program, which his teacher banned him from reading to the class on the grounds that the subject matter was "inappropriate."[70] He "tried to present the paper at a meeting of the local neo-Nazis, but it was too scholarly for his shaven-headed, beer-swilling audience."[71] After that, he limited himself to his website, where under the codename "Wilhelm" he presented Gustloff as an authentic German hero and repeated his grandmother's claim that the "Kraft durch Freude" cruise ships demonstrated true socialism at work.

Before long, Konrad provoked an angry response. Calling himself "David," this adversary insisted that Gustloff's assassin, David Frankfurter, was the hero, a hero of the Jewish resistance. A contest of words in virtual space ensues. But that does not satisfy Konrad. He invites "David"—who turns out to be his own age—to meet. At the story's climax, the two boys come face to face at Gustloff's grave, and Konrad shoots "David." Only after the murder does the reader learn that "David" was in fact, as Tulla puts it, "a fake Yid." Konrad is unmoved by this revelation. At his trial, he says, "I shot because I am a German—and because the eternal Jew spoke through David."[72] Cross-examined, he admits that he has never encountered a real Jew.

During a recess in the trial, Paul and his ex-wife, Gabi, have a "frank conversation" with the parents of Wolfgang, alias David. Paul brings up, "in a fairly confused fashion," the oral report that had been banned in his son's school.

> Immediately Gabi and I were fighting again, just as we had eons ago during our marriage. I argued that our son's unhappiness—and its dreadful consequences—started when he was prohibited from presenting his view of 30 January 1933, and also the social significance of the Nazi organization Strength through Joy, but Gabi interrupted me: "Perfectly understandable that the teacher had put a stop to it. After all, in terms of that date, its real significance was that it was the day of Hitler's takeover, not that it happened to be the birthday of a minor figure—[Gustloff was born on January 30, 1895]—about whose importance our son wanted to go on and on.[73]

If Konrad had been allowed to read his paper in class, Paul seems to suggest, he would not have become a neo-Nazi. And if the past had been discussed in a way that empathized with the motives of Hitler's followers, the boy would not have become a killer.

What about Wolfgang, the actual victim? His mother was of the view that he had "always been an oddball."

> [R]elatively early, at the age of fourteen, her son adopted the name David and became so obsessed with thoughts of atonement for the wartime atrocities and mass killings, which, God knows, were constantly harped on in our society, that eventually everything Jewish became somehow sacred to him …. And it had been … off-putting to see him sitting in his room at his … computer, wearing one of those little caps Jews wore.

She continued:

> It was … dreadful what happened when that ship went down. All those children. We didn't know anything about it. Not even my husband, and his hobby is research on recent German history. Even he didn't have any information on the Gustloff case.

If Wolfgang has been raised on what had "happened when the ship went down," his mother implies, he would not have "become so obsessed with thoughts of atonement."[74]

Would the knowledge that Germans, too, had endured enormous suffering, would that knowledge have led Wolfgang to "identify himself," as Hillgruber urged, "with the concrete fate of the German population in the East?" Would that knowledge have led him to ignore—to turn a blind eye to—what Germans had done to Jews?

4

From Holodomor to Holocaust

With the inauguration of the Berlin Holocaust memorial in 2005, the narrative of Germans killing Jews had been enshrined. The historian Eberhard Jäckel, who, along with Lea Rosh, spearheaded the drive to build the memorial, certainly thought so. He claimed that the Nazi "murder of the Jews was unique because never before had a nation with the authority of its leader decided and announced that it would kill off as completely as possible a particular group of humans ... and actually put this decision into practice, using all the means of governmental power at its disposal." To prove his point, he went on to quote Reichsführer-SS, Heinrich Himmler: "The question was posed to us: What about the women and children? I have decided to find a clear solution here, too. I ... did not feel justified in exterminating the men (that is, killing them or having them killed)—and allowing avengers in the form of little children to grow up for our sons and grandsons. We had to come to the grave decision to make this people disappear from the face of the earth."[1] Jäckel made these remarks in the midst of the Historikerstreit, the German historians' controversy, a controversy that had threatened the growing consensus before it could be cast in concrete.[2]

The *Historikerstreit* started in mid-1986 with an article by the philosopher Jürgen Habermas in the influential weekly *Die Zeit*. In it, he challenged Ernst Nolte, a historian, known for his penchant for proposing a causal connection between Bolshevism and Nazism. Defensive briefs for Nolte were quick to appear, and these, in turn, became the targets of criticism. By year's end, nearly every major historian in the country had had something to say, with liberal-minded scholars considered to be the victors.[3]

Given this outcome, it is surprising that Nolte's claim that the Soviets and Nazis taught and enabled each other should have been revived. But so it was. Twenty-five years after the *Historikerstreit*, the Yale historian Timothy Snyder published *Bloodlands*.[4] Both Stalin and Hitler, Snyder asserted, began by trying to implement unreachable goals: the very rapid collectivization of agriculture, mainly in Ukraine, and the creation of German-occupied Lebensraum [living space] in Eastern Europe. Both programs failed, and both dictators blamed others for their failure, Stalin, above all, kulaks and Ukrainians and Poles, while Hitler singled out Jews. And both vented their anger by killing these people in the millions.

Neither Nolte nor Snyder denied the presence of anti-Semitism. They did, however, marginalize it. They thus opened up the prospect of writing the history of the Holocaust without anti-Semitism as its central feature. The crime might be memorialized, but the crucial motive for it would be missing.

I. The *Historikerstreit*

A philosopher by training and profession, who taught at the University of Frankfurt, Habermas was also at home in the fields of history and sociology. And in English as well. He had taught in the United States and was appreciative of Western liberalism. For Habermas, "democracy, for all its failings, figured as a basic given—at the very least a point of departure for deep structural reform."[5]

At the outset of what became the *Historikerstreit*, Habermas defended the public role of the intellectual, and he did so based on a conception of citizenship—democratic and anti-technocratic. He insisted that "the arena, in which none of us can be nonparticipants, should not be confused with discussion among … scholars …. Prissy indignation about the ostensible conflation of politics and scholarship puts the issue on a false basis." He made his case with a series of rhetorical questions:

> Can one become the legal successor to the German Reich and continue the traditions of German culture without taking on historical liability for the form of life in which Auschwitz was possible? Is there any way to bear the liability for the context in which such crimes originated, a context with which one's own existence is historically interwoven, other than through remembrance … of what cannot be made good … [and] through a reflexive, scrutinizing attitude toward one's own identity-forming traditions? Can we not say that … the more … a collective context of life … has maintained itself externally through the … destruction of life that is alien to it, the greater is the burden of … critical self-examination … imposed on … subsequent generations? And does not this very thesis forbid us to use leveling comparisons to play down the fact that no one can take our place in the liability required of us?[6]

What incensed Habermas was Nolte's attempt to play off Nazi crimes against those of other regimes and periods—his "macabre reckonings of damages."[7]

Nolte's revisionist interpretation amounted to a denial of what is meant to be German after Auschwitz.

* * * * * * * * * * *

One of the most brilliant, and certainly the most brooding, German thinker about the recent past, Nolte had studied with the philosopher Martin Heidegger. He made his mark as a historian with *Der Faschismus in seiner Epoche* (*Three Faces of Fascism*). It appeared in 1963, and in it, he argued that the merely protofascist *Action Française* deserved equal billing with the Italian and German movements. A decade later he published *Deutschland und der kalte Krieg* (*Germany and the Cold War*), a far more problematic work.[8] He "called for a historical sense that could rehabilitate the reputation of the old Bismarckian Reich and recognize that every major nation (Britain and the United States excepted) has had 'its own Hitler era, with its monstrosities and sacrifices.'"[9]

In an article entitled "The Past That Will Not Pass," Nolte put bluntly his principal claim:

> It is a notable shortcoming that the literature about National Socialism does not know or does not want to admit to what degree all the deeds—with the single exception of the technical process of gassing—that the National Socialists later committed had already been described in the voluminous literature of the 1920s: mass deportations and executions, torture, death camps, the extermination of entire groups using strictly objective selection criteria, and public demands for the annihilation of millions of guiltless people who were thought to be "enemies."[10]

Or as Joachim Fest, co-editor of the *Frankfurter Allgemeine Zeitung*, noted in a follow-up:

> The gas chambers with which the executors of the annihilation of the Jews went to work without a doubt signal a particularly repulsive form of mass murder and they have justifiably become a symbol for the technicized barbarism of the Hitler regime. But can it really be said that the mass liquidations by a bullet to the back of the neck, as was common practice during the years of the Red Terror, are qualitatively different? Isn't, despite all the differences, the comparable element stronger?[11]

The questions that were now permissible, even unavoidable, Nolte asserted, had become clear:

> Did the National Socialists or Hitler perhaps commit an "Asiatic" deed merely because they and their ilk considered themselves to be potential victims of an

"Asiatic" deed? Was the Gulag Archipelago not primary to Auschwitz? Was the Bolshevik murder of an entire class not the logical and factual prius of the "racial murder" of National Socialism?[12]

And the answers were equally clear:

> Auschwitz was the fear-borne reaction to the acts of annihilation that took place during the Russian Revolution …. [T]he so-called annihilation of the Jews by the Third Reich was a … distorted copy and not a first act or an original.[13]

In a letter to Nolte, the eminent French historian François Furet underlined what logically followed:

> [H]ow can your insistence on the secondary and derivative character of Nazism vis-à-vis Bolshevism *not* be seen as an attempt to exonerate the former by indicting the latter? If Nazi crimes are contained in a response to Bolshevik crimes, they thereby obviously acquire a no less criminal character but a less deliberate one and … a less *primary* one.[14]

* * * * * * * * * * *

Saul Friedländer, who later wrote the magisterial *Nazi Germany and the Jews*,[15] had his own bizarre encounter with Nolte. He had read *Three Faces of Fascism* and had, in fact, assigned it in courses. So in early 1986, months before the *Historikerstreit* took off, Friedländer, on sabbatical in Berlin, accepted Nolte's invitation to a small dinner party.

As the company sat down to the table, Friedländer "felt almost completely at ease …. Soup was served, and in the momentary silence," Nolte turned to him.

> "Herr Friedländer, you cannot deny that there is something like world Jewry [*Weltjudentum*]."
>
> "How so?"
>
> "Well, isn't there a World Jewish Congress?"
>
> I tried to explain why and when the World Jewish Congress had been established. It didn't help …. The sniping continued.
>
> "Didn't Weizmann declare, in September 1939, that world Jewry would fight on the side of Great Britain against Germany?" …
>
> "Indeed, [Chaim] Weizmann, [a leading Zionist], declared that Jews would fight against Nazi Germany. Not that this Zionist leader in any way represented Jews in different countries, but given the way the Third Reich was hounding the Jews and given the nature of the regime, he assumed quite rightly that Jews, wherever they lived, would be on the side of Great Britain."

> "But, Herr Friedländer, didn't it mean that World Jewry was thereby at war with Germany and thus that Hitler could consider Jews as enemies and intern them in concentration camps as prisoners of war, as the Americans did with the Japanese?"
>
> So it went. Everybody was silent around us. Nolte was red in the face and I was pale, or perhaps it was the other way around. The soup was cold. My host carefully added, "Concentration camps, not extermination camps." The entire situation was becoming unbearable .... I got up and asked for a taxi .... At the door, I told Nolte that where I come from, one did not invite people to dinner in order to insult them.

As Friedländer was preparing to leave Berlin, *Die Zeit* interviewed him about his stay in the German capital. He "mentioned some of the views a well-known historian was peddling around."[16] He did not give a name, but shortly after publication, Nolte announced that he was the historian in question.

* * * * * * * * * * *

Ten years after the *Historikerstreit* had calmed down, the first volume of Friedländer's *Nazi Germany and the Jews* appeared in print. In the opening pages, he made clear what he sought to accomplish. He aimed at an integrated account—one in which Nazi practices were the "central element," but one in which the wider society as well as the victims' attitudes and fortunes was no less crucial. Though he basically followed "the chronological sequence of events"— the first volume detailing the prewar period—he also resorted to sudden narrative shifts. These abrupt moves allowed him to "juxtapose entirely different levels of reality—for example, high level anti-Jewish policy debates ... next to routine scenes of persecution."[17]

The depravity of the Nazi regime, he insisted, would not be found in any German documents. It could be caught only in the "voice-over of the victims."[18] Time and time again, he tuned into the words of Victor Klemperer, who before the Nazis came to power had been a professor of Romance languages and literature at Dresden Technical University and who managed to survive the war, thanks to his marriage to, in Nazi jargon, a "full-blood Aryan." Her "racial purity" exempted him from deportation to the East and almost certain death.[19]

In *LTI (Lingua tertii imperii,* 1947), Klemperer's philological analysis of how the Nazis corrupted the German language and in so doing corrupted German thought, he reported on a run-in with the Gestapo. Ordered off a tram, marched to Gestapo headquarters, thoroughly searched—nothing prohibited was found on him—he was set free.

> I already had my hand on the door when he [the policeman] calls me back: "At home you're all praying for the Jewish victory, aren't you. Don't gawp at me like that, and don't answer either, because I know you do. It's your war—what? You're shaking your head? Who are we at war with then? Open your mouth when you are asked a question, you're supposed to be a professor aren't you?"—"With England, France and Russia, with … "—"Oh shut up, that's a load of rubbish. We're at war with the Jews, it's the Jewish war. And if you shake your head once more I'll hit you so hard you'll have to go straight to the dentist. It's the Jewish war, the Führer said so, and the Führer is always right."[20]

Reflecting on Nazi linguistic practices, Klemperer continued:

> *Der Jude–* … even more common … is the adjective *"jüdisch* [Jewish]*,"* because it is the adjective above all which has the bracketing effect of binding together all adversaries into a single enemy: the Jewish-Marxist *Weltanschauung*, the Jewish-Bolshevist philistinism, the Jewish-Capitalist system of exploitation, the keen Jewish-English, Jewish-American interest in seeing Germany destroyed: thus from 1933 every single hostility, regardless of its origin, can be traced back to one and the same enemy, Hitler's hidden maggot, the Jew.[21]

As for Nolte, in his post-*Historikerstreit, Der europäische Bürgerkrieg* (*The European Civil War*),[22] he "came to portray Hitler as the protector of the European bourgeoisie against the threat represented by Bolshevism." Friedländer asked the obvious question: Why then exterminate the Jews? The answer Nazi propaganda offered—and Klemperer registered—was that "Jews were the initiators and carriers of Bolshevism." Nolte, Friedländer quipped, "was careful enough not to use this argument."[23]

II. Variations on a Theme

Bloodlands, published in 2010, was a huge success, reaching an audience worldwide. It made it onto bestseller lists in six countries, including the United States, Germany, and Poland. It was translated into thirty-three languages. The praise was lavish. Among the many distinctions it racked up was the Leipzig Book Prize for European Understanding and one named in honor of Hannah Arendt. Snyder, so the committee for the latter prize claimed, by focusing on the horrors in Eastern Europe, had shed new light on the Second World War. And the Foundation for Polish Science concurred when it presented Snyder with its award—the highest scientific accolade in Poland.

Until now, Snyder wrote, there has been no history of Europe between Hitler and Stalin; there has been no history of what he labeled the bloodlands, extending from central Poland to western Russia, through Ukraine, Belarus, and the Baltic states. The bloodlands "were no political territory, real or imagined; they are simply where Europe's most murderous regimes did their most murderous work."[24]

Numbers helped tell the story. "In the middle of Europe in the middle of the twentieth century, the Nazi and Soviet regimes murdered some fourteen million people." They "were murdered over the course of ... twelve years, between 1933 and 1945, while both Hitler and Stalin were in power. Though their homelands became battlefields midway through this period, these people were all victims of murderous policy rather than casualties of war .... [N]ot a single one ... was a soldier on active duty. Most were women, children, and the aged; none were [sic] bearing weapons, many had been stripped of their possessions, including their clothes."[25]

"Of the fourteen million people deliberately murdered in the bloodlands between 1933 and 1945," Snyder wrote, "a third belong in the Soviet account." Before 1939, Stalin's record of mass murder was far more "imposing" than Hitler's. In the name of defending and modernizing the Soviet Union, he oversaw "the starvation of millions and the shooting of three quarters of a million people." He "killed his own citizens, no less efficiently than Hitler killed the citizens of other countries." With the outbreak of the Second World War—or, as Snyder put it, "after Stalin allowed Hitler to begin a war"— German policies of mass murder came to rival those of the Soviets. "The Wehrmacht and the Red Army both attacked Poland in September 1939, ... and German and Soviet forces occupied the country together for nearly two years .... Both regimes shot educated Polish citizens in the tens of thousands and deported them in the hundreds of thousands. For Stalin, such mass repression was the continuation of old policies on new lands; for Hitler, it was a breakthrough."[26]

Snyder harped on similarities between the two regimes; he drew parallels between them. But *Bloodlands* is structured to suggest that more than likeness was involved, that, as Nolte and Fest had argued, Stalin set the pace and Hitler followed suit. Discussing anti-Jewish pogroms that followed on the heels of Hitler's invasion of the Soviet Union on June 22, 1941, Snyder claimed that they "took place where the Soviets had recently arrived and where Soviet power was recently installed, where for the previous months Soviet organs of coercion had organized arrests, executions, and deportations. They were a joint production, a Nazi edition of a Soviet text."²⁷

* * * * * * * * * *

Beginning in the 1930s, Stalin undertook an unprecedented agricultural experiment in Ukraine: he collectivized the land and conducted a "war" against the kulaks, the "wealthy" peasants—whose wealth sometimes consisted of a single cow.

Known as "the breadbasket of Europe," Ukraine's rich black soil has produced grain for international trade since the days of Herodotus. Without Ukrainian grain, the Bolshevik regime was doomed. In the 1920s, the Soviet Union survived civil war and economic collapse by making concessions to the Ukrainian peasantry and to Ukrainian nationalism: the New Economic Policy allowed peasants to keep the land they had acquired during the revolution and introduced elements of a market economy, and Ukrainization promised support for the Ukrainian language and culture in exchange for giving up aspirations to political sovereignty. The Bolsheviks considered both policies nothing more than temporary expedients.

By the end of the decade, Stalin was determined to change course, to accelerate the revolutionary transformation of the economy and society. The Bolshevik leaders' hopes that the Russian Revolution would ignite world revolution, first in Europe and then in the colonial East, had never materialized and had been replaced by the resolve to build socialism in one country—their own. To survive in a hostile capitalist environment, so they reasoned, they needed a strong industrial base and an ideology with deeper local roots than Marxist internationalism. They looked to villages to provide resources for industrialization and to Russian nationalism to provide legitimization. Both boded ill for Ukraine.

His policy of forced collectivization, implemented in the fall of 1929, would, Stalin argued, "'colonize' [Soviet] peasants: squeeze them harder and invest this 'internal accumulation' into ... industry."²⁸ He singled out Ukraine for especially rapid conversion to the supposedly more efficient model of agriculture. Those who questioned the new policy were declared to be kulaks, and eventually the regime began to apply the term to almost anyone who opposed its rule. The goal was to remove the potential opponents of collectivization from an important grain-producing area and soften the peasant resistance to government policies. As Snyder wrote:

> In the first four months of 1930, 113,637 people were forcibly transported from Soviet Ukraine as kulaks. Such an action meant about thirty thousand huts emptied one after another, their surprised inhabitants given little time to prepare for the unknown. It meant thousands of freezing freight cars, filled with terrified and sick human cargo, bound for destinations in northern European Russia, the Urals, Siberia, or Kazakhstan. It meant gun shots and cries of terror at the last dawn peasants would see at home; it meant frostbite and humiliation on the trains, and anguish and resignation as peasants disembarked as slave laborers on the taiga or the steppe.[29]

And still the Ukrainian villages resisted. Outright refusal was often followed by immediate action. Ordered to hand over their livestock to collective farms they did not trust, peasants began to slaughter cows, pigs, sheep, and even horses. They ate the meat, salted it, sold it, or concealed it—anything to prevent the collective farms from getting hold of it.[30] In an article dated March 2, 1930, with the curious title "Dizzy with Success," Stalin sounded a retreat. He resorted to the well-tried trick of shifting the blame to subordinates who had "misunderstood" his directions. For the next few months, collectivization proceeded more slowly. "In spring 1930, peasants in Ukraine harvested the winter wheat and saved the seeds for the autumn crops, just as if the land belonged to them."[31] The harvest of 1930 set a record.

"The temperate language of Stalin's ... article turned out to be just that: language."[32] All through the subsequent autumn sowing and winter harvest, and the following year's spring sowing and summer harvest, pressure on the peasants continued. Stalin moved his shock troops of party and Young Communist activists and secret police officers back into the countryside to push once more for collectivization. Threatened by violence, hundreds of thousands of peasants finally relinquished their land, animals, and machines. The grain they now sowed and harvested was requisitioned by the authorities, and they, in turn, worked as little as possible and produced much less than they could have done. The 1931 harvest was smaller than that of the previous year, not larger as Stalin had expected.

The failure of the first, collectivized, harvest was obvious. "Everybody understood, at some level, that collectivization was itself the source of the new shortages." But Stalin "had staked his leadership of the party on collectivization and he had defeated his rivals in the course of fighting for it. He could not be wrong." So he opted for coercion: "collective farms that had not met their grain quotas would have to repay any outstanding loans, and return any tractors or other equipment that had been leased to them .... Their spare cash—including that intended to buy seeds—would be confiscated."[33] In the spring of 1932, desperate officials began to collect grain wherever and however they could. This, despite their appreciation that famine was on its way.

As hunger spread, many were too weak to work in the fields, only about two-thirds of which were cultivated that spring. The food supply was clearly going to drop. Stalin, wrote Snyder, could have saved millions of lives. "He could have suspended food exports for a few months, released grain reserves ... , or given peasants access to local grain storage areas. Such simple measures, pursued as late as November 1932, could have kept the death toll to the hundreds of thousands rather than the millions. Stalin pursued none of them."

> In the waning weeks of 1932, ... with no conceivable justification other than to prove the inevitability of his rule, Stalin chose to kill millions of people in Soviet Ukraine. He shifted to a position of pure malice, where the Ukrainian peasant was somehow the aggressor and he, Stalin, the victim. Hunger was a form of aggression, ... against which starvation was the only defense. Stalin seemed determined to display his dominance over the Ukrainian peasantry, and seemed to enjoy the depths of suffering that such a posture would require.[34]

Stalin's malevolence amounted to a death sentence for more than 3 million in Ukraine—Snyder's figure[35]; a recent estimate has raised the number to nearly 4 million. Émigré publications, both at the time and later, described the famine of 1932–3 as "the *Holodomor*, a term derived from the Ukrainian word for hunger—*holod*—and extermination—*mor*."[36]

As the peasants starved to death, Stalin and his henchmen intensified their war on the Ukrainian intellectual and political class. They launched a campaign of slander against "professors, museum curators, writers, artists, priests, theologians, public officials and bureaucrats. Anyone connected to the short-lived Ukrainian People's Republic, which had existed for a few months ... [in 1917–8], anyone who had promoted the Ukrainian language or Ukrainian history, anyone with an independent literary or artistic career, was liable to be publicly vilified, jailed, sent to a labour camp or executed."[37] The Holodomor and the attack on the Ukrainian intelligentsia and political élite, taken together, neutered the Ukrainian national idea and any challenge to Soviet unity.

What happened in Ukraine does not easily conform to the definition of genocide set out in the United Nations convention of 1948, that is, "acts committed with intent to destroy, in whole or in part, a national, ethnical, racial or religious group, as such." It does, however, readily fit the definition furnished by Raphael Lemkin, the Polish-Jewish lawyer, who coined the term. He considered the Ukrainian case "the classic example." It was an instance "of destruction, not of individuals only, but of a culture and a nation."[38] Snyder agreed: "Hundreds of thousands of orphans would grow up to be Soviet citizens but not Ukrainians, at least not in the way that an intact Ukrainian family and a Ukrainian countryside might have made them."[39]

* * * * * * * * * * *

"The most persecuted European ... minority in the second half of the 1930s," Snyder declared, "was not the four hundred thousand or so German Jews (the number declining because of emigration) but the six hundred thousand or so Soviet Poles (the number declining because of executions)." Stalin, not Hitler, led the way—he "was a pioneer in national mass murder"—and "Poles were the preeminent victims among Soviet nationalities."[40]

Ethnic deportations began in the western border regions in 1935. The targets were diaspora nationalities, that is, national minorities with cross-border ethnic ties to a foreign nation-state. Leningrad fell within this zone, and there too western national minorities were swept up in a wave of persecution—Finns, Latvians, Estonians, Germans, Poles. By 1936, the Soviet Union's western diaspora nationalities had been stigmatized as collectively disloyal and subjected to ethnic cleansing.[41]

With the onset of the Great Terror in the summer of 1937, the national operations—the NKVD spoke of the German, the Latvian, the Finnish, and the Polish operations—merged with the large-scale purge of the Communist party. As for the Poles, on August 11, Nicolai Yezhov, chief of the NKVD, issued order 00485: it mandated the "total liquidation of the network of spies of the [supposed] Polish Military Organization"[42]—former prisoners of war who had remained in the Soviet Union after the Russo-Polish War of 1919–20, Polish emigrants, members of Polish political parties, and Polish populations in the Soviet Union's western border zones. Within weeks of its launch, Yezhov gave local NKVD posts the order to exclude "all Poles." "'The Poles have to be completely annihilated.' Whomever the NKVD identified as a Polish agent lost his freedom or his life."[43]

The national operations did not proceed without a hitch. "By September 1938 more than one hundred thousand cases awaited attention. As a result 'special troikas' were created to read files at a local level. They were composed of a local party head, a local NKVD chief, and a local prosecutor.... Considering hundreds of cases a day, going through the backlog in about six weeks, the special troikas sentenced about 72,000 people to death .... In the Zhytomyr region in the far west of Soviet Ukraine near Poland, a troika sentenced ... 100 people to death on 22 September 1938, then another 138 on the following day, and then another 408 on 28 September."[44]

According to Snyder's calculations, 143,810 people were accused of espionage for Poland; of these, 111,091 were executed. "Not all of them were Poles, but most of them were. ... Taking into account the number of deaths, the percentage of death sentences to arrests, the risk of arrest, ethnic Poles suffered more than any other group within the Soviet Union during the Great Terror. By a conservative estimate, some eighty-five thousand Poles were executed in 1937 and 1938, which means that one-eighth of the 681,692 mortal victims of the Great Terror were Polish."[45]

What about the Nazi oppression of the Jews in the 1930s? Kristallnacht merited a mere paragraph. Only "a few hundred Jews were killed," though, to be sure, "thousands of shops and hundreds of synagogues [were] destroyed." Nothing compared to the slaughter of the Great Terror. And, indeed, with the joint German-Soviet invasion of Poland, "Hitler, like Stalin, would choose Poles as the target" for his first campaign of mass murder.[46]

* * * * * * * * * * *

Poland experienced both regimes. The Soviets and the Germans did not simply occupy but rather sought to subjugate, exploit, and integrate their portions of Poland into their empires. The Soviet Union enlarged its Ukrainian and Belorussian republics, and in June 1940, it annexed all three independent Baltic States: Estonia, Latvia, and Lithuania. Nazi Germany claimed the western Polish territories as Warthegau and Reichsgau Danzig-West Prussia and immediately started "Germanizing" them. "In the end," Snyder claimed, "Soviet and German policies were very similar, with more or less concurrent deportations and more or less concurrent mass shootings."[47]

In eastern Poland, after a few weeks of chaos, the Soviets imposed their own institutions: now everyone had to register for an internal passport; now the state had a record of all of its new citizens. "Registration ... allowed for the smooth pursuit of a major Soviet policy: deportation." There were four major deportations: February, April, June 1940, and June 1941. Snyder paid special attention to the first of these. It included "groups of Polish citizens deemed to pose a danger to the new order: military veterans, foresters, civil servants, policemen, and their families."

> [O]n one evening in February 1940, in temperatures of about forty below zero [Celsius], the NKVD gathered all of them: 139,794 people taken from their homes at night at gunpoint to unequipped freight trains bound for special settlements in distant Soviet Kazakhstan or Siberia .... Food and water were given very irregularly, and the cattle cars were without facilities and extremely cold .... [T]he trains were full of aged parents as well as the children of people who were thought to be dangerous. At halts on the journey east, guards would go from car to car, asking if there were any dead children .... During the passage alone, some five thousand people would die; about eleven thousand more would perish by the following summer .... Even more than the kulaks who had preceded them [to the forced labor zones], these Poles were alien and helpless in central Asia or the Russian north.[48]

And then there were those murdered outright. The Soviets took more than one hundred thousand prisoners of war. They released the men and held onto the officers, most of whom came from the reserves. They were "educated professionals and intellectuals, ... doctors, lawyers, scientists, professors, and politicians." In April 1940, the prisoners, who had been kept in three different camps, were taken by rail to execution sites. "In all, this lesser Terror, this revival of the Polish operation, killed 21,892 Polish citizens. The vast majority of whom, though not all, were Poles by nationality." The slaughter of these men "was a kind of decapitation of Polish society."[49]

This decapitation fitted very nicely with German plans. In Operation Tannenberg—the name evoked the victory of the German armies over Russian forces in 1914—some 60,000 Poles whose names had been collected over the prewar years were to be eliminated. But, according to Snyder, the Einsatzgruppen charged with this task "lacked the experience and thus the skills of the NKVD. They killed civilians, to be sure, often under the cover of retaliatory operations against supposed partisans." Fifty thousand Polish citizens were put to death "in actions that had nothing to do with combat. But these were not, it seems, the first fifty thousand on their list ... Unlike the NKVD, the Einsatzgruppen did not follow protocols carefully, and in Poland did not keep careful records of the people they killed."[50]

The resettlement of ethnic Germans from Soviet territories—another top priority—entailed the expulsion of Poles from the Warthegau to the General

Government, the area of central Poland that Germany had not annexed. Polish farmers had to be deported "to make room for these incoming Germans." The first deportation took place in December 1939, the second and third in February and March of the following year. The total number of people removed was more than 130,000. "The journey was rather short. In normal times, the … [trip] from Poznań, the capital of the Warthegau, to Warsaw, the largest city in the General Government, would take a few hours. Nevertheless, thousands of people froze to death on the trains, which were often left on the tracks for days."[51] The remaining Polish population was to be exploited as slave laborers.

As for the Jewish population, from the beginning, Jews were persecuted, humiliated, mistreated, and murdered. Snyder ignored the gratuitous cruelty involved; Friedländer did not:

> [T]orturing … [Jews] offered welcome enjoyment to both soldiers and SS personnel. The choice victims were Orthodox Jews, given their distinctive looks and attire. They were shot at; they were compelled to smear feces on each other; they had to jump, crawl, sing, clean excrement with prayer shawls, dance around bonfires of burning Torah scrolls. They were whipped, forced to eat pork, or had Jewish stars carved on their foreheads. The "beard game" was the most popular entertainment of all: Beards and sidelocks were shorn, plucked, torn, set afire, hacked off with or without parts of skin, cheeks, or jaws, to the amusement of a usually large audience of cheering soldiers. On Yom Kippur 1939 such entertainment for the troops was particularly lively.[52]

Both Nazi Germany and the Soviet Union—like Prussia and Tsarist Russia in the nineteenth century—could have profited from the Polish partition for decades. But Hitler clung to his plan to conquer Lebensraum in the East by means of war. After an invasion of Britain—following triumphant campaigns against Denmark, Norway, the Netherlands, Belgium, and especially France—had been called off, he returned to his old plans of attacking the Soviet Union. In the period 1941–5, Nazi Germany clearly became dominant in mass murder.

* * * * * * * * * *

"Hitler's utopias crumbled on contact with the Soviet Union." Snyder counted four of them: "a Hunger Plan that would starve thirty million people in months; … a Generalplan Ost that would make of the western Soviet Union a German colony; … a Final Solution that would eliminate European Jewry after the war; … [and] a lightning victory that would destroy the Soviet Union in weeks."[53]

When the Wehrmacht failed to smash the Red Army, the other three "utopias" had to be rejiggered.

"Collectivization," Snyder argued, "had brought starvation to Soviet Ukraine, first as an unintended result of inefficiencies and unrealistic grain targets, and then as an intended consequence of the vengeful extractions of late 1932 and early 1933. Hitler, on the other hand, *planned in advance* to starve unwanted Soviet populations to death."[54] In the weeks before Operation Barbarossa was launched, economic experts outlined a scenario of mass starvation and massive exploitation. The authors of a set of guidelines proposed radically restructuring the Soviet economy by siphoning off food from Ukraine and parts of southern Russia for the benefit of German troops, German civilians, and the rest of German-dominated Europe. The population in the south, as producers of agricultural surplus, might hope to have the bare minimum for subsistence; those in the north, the so-called "hunger zone," which included the industrial areas of Moscow and Leningrad, had little chance of surviving. The guidelines envisioned millions disappearing, either by death through starvation or through the "evacuation" of "superfluous eaters."[55]

The war did not go as Hitler and his henchmen expected, and the Wehrmacht could not implement the Hunger Plan as originally designed. Nonetheless millions of Soviet citizens were purposely starved. Army Group South banned the supply of provisions to Kiev. "The logic was that the food in the countryside was to remain there, to be collected by the army and then later by a German civilian authority." Army Group North laid mines around Leningrad with the object of starving the city out of existence. "By end of the siege in 1944, about one million people had lost their lives."[56] And at least three and a third million Soviet prisoners of war were deliberately killed in German captivity, allowed to die of starvation, illness, and neglect, or simply shot.

The Hunger Plan dovetailed with the Generalplan Ost—commissioned by Himmler the day before the invasion of the Soviet Union. Within weeks he had an initial draft and within a year he had the final version. The Plan "proposed to remove between 80 and 85 percent of the Polish population, 64 percent of the Ukrainian and 75 percent of the Belorussian, expelling them further east or allowing them to perish from disease and malnutrition"—in total somewhere between 30 and 45 million Slavs.[57] The space vacated by the Slavs would, then, be occupied by 10 million Germans. "Had the German invasion proceeded as envisioned, as a lightning victory that leveled the great Soviet cities and yielded Ukrainian food and Caucasian oil," the Germans would have gone ahead with Generalplan Ost or some variant thereof.

Instead, their "fantasy scenario" of becoming a great land empire had to be shelved.[58]

As for eliminating the Jews from Europe, rather than being postponed to war's end, the notorious Final Solution was pushed up. Hitler had not originally aimed to kill all Jews. He and his chief lieutenants had canvassed other options. With over 2 million Jews in their half of Poland, Nazi leaders sketched out a "plan to create some sort of reservation for Jews in the Lublin district of the General Government." This was far from satisfactory: the "General Government was too near and too small," and Hans Frank, the governor-general, objected—"he had no wish for any more Jews in his colony." What was to be done? The Jews were to be segregated and exploited. From the outset, the ghettos were considered temporary means for controlling the Jewish population before its expulsion. In 1940 and 1941, "the Warsaw ghetto and the other ghettos became improvised labor camps and holding pens."[59]

The Lublin plan was too obviously unrealistic to have been considered for any length of time; so too the notion of deporting the Jews of Europe to Madagascar. The island was a French possession, and France had fallen. But the Royal Navy commanded the sea lanes and, thus, "prevented Hitler's oceanic version of the Final Solution."[60] If the Germans could not ferry a few hundred thousand troops across the Channel to attack Britain, how could they have deported millions of people to an island in the Indian Ocean?

Snyder was intent on denying that Nazi policy was heading toward the extermination of the Jews in the near, not distant, future. On this point, Friedländer did not beat about the bush:

> [Even] if ... the outlines of the "Final Solution" were not yet apparent on the eve of Barbarossa, Hitler had "clearly defined" the thrust of the campaign in March 1941: It was to be a war of extermination, and by definition mass murder would expand as long as the enemy was fighting, as long as enemies were still within reach. In other words, the Reich was now set on a path that at some point, under specific circumstances, within a particular context, would lead to the decision to exterminate all the Jews of Europe.[61]

The war against the Jews, Snyder insisted, was a response to the failure of the war against the Soviets—and that failure was amply apparent six months after the launch of Barbarossa. Here Snyder relied on the work of Christian Gerlach. It was frustration, Gerlach maintained, dating to Pearl Harbor and the Red Army's successful counterattack defending Moscow that prompted Hitler to decide on the annihilation of Europe's Jews.[62] Few historians have accepted Gerlach's contention. Christopher Browning, for one, has argued that the tipping point toward the Final Solution came months earlier, in September and October. In a moment of euphoria at the scale and rapidity of German victories, Hitler determined to give the order to kill the Jews. It was at this juncture that he chose to fulfill his "prophecy" of January 1939, that is, if Jews plunged the nations of the world into war, it was they who would be destroyed.[63]

What purpose did Snyder's insistence on the December date serve? (As to the timing of the decision, Friedländer felt under no obligation to choose between the competing views. He did argue that "crossing the line from local murder operations to overall extermination required a go-ahead signal from the supreme authority.")[64] To claim that the Holocaust was a consolation prize for the failure of Barbarossa and that Hitler knew by the end of 1941 that the war was lost—not a credible claim—meshed with Snyder's thesis that the killings of 1933–45 were parallel programs of mass murder, with Stalin setting an example for Hitler and/or goading him into action.

> After collectivization brought resistance and hunger to Soviet Ukraine, Stalin blamed kulaks and Ukrainians and Poles. After the Wehrmacht was halted at Moscow and the Americans entered the Second World War, Hitler blamed Jews. Just as the kulaks and Ukrainians and Poles had taken the blame for slowing the construction of the Soviet system, the Jews took the blame for preventing its destruction .... Stalin's interpretation was used to justify the starvation of kulaks and members of national minorities; Hitler's interpretation was used to justify the shooting and gassing of all Jews. After collectivization starved millions to death, this was adduced by Stalin to be evidence of a victorious class struggle. As the Jews were shot and then gassed, Hitler presented this, in ever clearer terms, as a war aim in itself. When the war was lost, Hitler called the mass murder of Jews his victory.[65]

* * * * * * * * * * * *

In Snyder's account, the 14 million replaced the proverbial 6 million. (His obsession with citing statistics down to the last digit in hard to square with the notorious unreliability of such figures.) Jewish losses no longer stood out as distinctive. And the hundreds of thousands of German and West European Jews who were killed rated little more than a page. By addressing the Holocaust almost exclusively in terms of Hitler's plans for Eastern Europe, and by drawing rhetorical parallels with the mass murders carried out in the same areas on Stalin's orders, Snyder minimized what was unique about the extermination of the Jews: the comprehensive European, even global, scale of the Nazis' intentions.

Snyder missed, or discounted, the extent of Nazi ambitions, and, by the same token, he overlooked the depth of the hatred and fear that drove it on. Friedländer, in contrast, brought anti-Jewish ideology into sharp relief. It "could be formulated ... in the tersest way: *The Jew was a lethal and active threat to all nations, to the Aryan race and to the German Volk.* The emphasis is not only on 'lethal' but also—and mainly—on 'active.' While all other groups targeted by the Nazi regime (the mentally ill, 'asocials' and homosexuals, 'inferior' racial groups including Gypsies and Slavs) were essentially *passive* threats (as long as the Slavs, for example, were not led by Jews), the Jews were the only group that, since its appearance in history, relentlessly plotted and maneuvered to subdue all of humanity."[66] It was these paranoid, and widely shared, fantasies that provided the context for the emergence of the Final Solution. Any explanation of the Holocaust as the by-product of Nazi policies geared toward resettlement and expansion, or by the need to solve immediate, local, pragmatic problems (such as food supply)—that is, which downplays the ideology of the perpetrators—is wide of the mark.

III. Coda

Snyder portrayed the Nazi decision-making process as far more clear-cut than most historians now think it was—and reduced it to very small number of actors, essentially Hitler and a few others. According to him, when Operation Barbarossa did not go as expected, and Hitler "reformulated the war aims such that the physical extermination of the Jews became the priority," Himmler showed "how it could be achieved." He "ignored what was impossible, pondered what was most glorious, and did what could be done: kill the Jews ... in occupied eastern Poland, the Baltic States, and the Soviet Union." Hitler "was the leader, and his henchmen owed their positions to their ability to divine and realize 'his will.'"[67] In short, Snyder turned exterminationist policy into a vying for Hitler's favor.

In focusing on Hitler's role, Snyder turned a blind eye to the fact that the Germans were welcomed by much of the native populations. No credible historian would argue that without the massive assistance and active participation of homegrown perpetrators, the Holocaust would have been of the magnitude it was. (Characteristically, Snyder did not even mention the murderous pogrom by Poles of their Jewish neighbors in Jedwabne in July 1941.) In his narrative, the occupied populations were largely victims; they were nothing but helpless pawns. Which underlines the most glaring omission of *Bloodlands*: the role of local collaborators in the genocide of European Jewry.

5

Revising History, Reviving Nationalism

In the Hungarian film *1945*, which opened in 2017, two Orthodox Jews arrive by train and slowly walk down the dusty road toward the village. They follow behind a horse-drawn buckboard that carries their two mysterious wooden trunks. The purpose of their journey is obscure, and they barely speak. The stationmaster bicycles ahead to warn the villagers, who start talking among themselves and jump to the conclusion that the black-clad strangers are connected to deported Jews. "We have to give it all back," the village drunk insists. His steely wife opts, instead, to hide her newly acquired rugs and silverware. "If anyone asks, the stuff isn't here, the Germans took it—or the Russians." The film gradually reveals how the village's veneer of civility covers over treachery and thievery. Now trailing behind the two Jews, the villagers watch in amazement as the strangers open the trunks, take out prayer shawls, and carefully make up bundles of assorted objects, including a child's shoes, and bury them in a newly dug grave. These objects were all that was left. Then the two Jews retrace their steps and make their way back to the train station.

The atmosphere is one of menace—the viewer assumes that the Jews are in jeopardy. And so Jews were who dared to show up at their former homes. In Hungary there were anti-Jewish demonstrations and attacks on individual Jews in 1946. The worst and bloodiest took place in Kunmadaras against the small number of Jewish survivors—seventy-three out of a prewar Jewish population of 250. Rumors spread that Jews made sausages out of Christian children—the blood libel was obviously alive and well—and that in a nearby town, several Christian children had gone missing. The crowd assaulted local Jews, killing two and wounding fifteen.[1]

In Poland, the plight of returning Jews was even worse. The hostility to Jews in postwar Poland was everywhere. Between the August 1945 pogrom in Kraków and the July 1946 pogrom in Kielce, the figures for the number of Jews murdered range from 500 to 1,000. Jews were in danger at work, in government offices, in classrooms, in the street—and especially in trains. "Time and again, returning

Jews were greeted … on arrival … in their native towns with an incredulous: 'So'—followed by the first name, as they were usually on a first-name basis with their Polish neighbors—'you are still alive?' … [B]efore long they got an unambiguous hint, or a piece of good advice—to clear out, or else."[2]

The most notorious pogrom took place in Kielce. When an eight-year-old boy hitched a ride to see former playmates in a village twenty-five kilometers from home and failed to come back that night, his father reported his disappearance to the police. Two days later, the boy turned up safe and sound. That should have been the end of the matter. It was not. The boy's father claimed that his son had been kidnapped by Jews and had managed to escape. A crowd gathered, shouting that Jews had killed a Christian child. Over the next twelve hours, in a couple of waves of violence, forty-two Jews were killed and eighty others injured. The hospital itself, to which Jews were transported, proved no safe haven. The wounded were at risk from other patients and medical personnel alike—though probably none was actually murdered.[3]

Jews fled from Hungary and Poland. At the end of the war, only 140,000 Jews were still in Hungary, down from 800,000 in 1941. (Many Jews liberated outside Hungary never returned.) Between 1945 and 1954, 40,000–50,000 immigrated, mostly to Israel. After the Hungarian Revolution of 1956, another 20,000 or so left the country. Yet, in 2010, with a population of approximately 100,000, Hungary had the highest number of Jews of any former Soviet satellite. And Poland had just about the lowest. More than 90 percent of the 3.5 million Jews who lived in Poland before 1939 perished in the Holocaust. The postwar Jewish population peaked briefly at around 250,000 in the summer of 1946. To the very small number who had survived in Poland itself was added the roughly 200,000 Polish Jews (no one knows exactly how many) who, during the period of the Nazi-Soviet nonaggression pact, had been deported or fled to the Soviet Union. "As perverse irony of Jewish fate would have it, victims of deportation turned out to be the lucky ones."[4] In the years immediately following the war, something like 160,000 Jews exited Poland. A second wave of emigration took place between 1957 and 1959. A third wave in 1968, prompted by the removal of Jews from party and state positions, left only a tiny community of Jews to survive the collapse of communism, in 1989.

From Stalin's death in 1953 until 1967, anti-Semitism, though endemic in Eastern Europe and the Soviet Union, was kept out of official Communist rhetoric. That changed with the Six-Day War between Israel and its Arab neighbors. Soviet support for the Arab cause legitimized vocal criticism of Israel, Zionism—and Jews. The Hungarian press published articles condemning Israeli expansion, but the tone remained moderate.[5] Unlike venomous Polish attacks, where party apparatchiks drew distinctions "between 'good' Communists with national Polish interests at heart and others (Jews) whose true affiliation lay elsewhere." And "newspapers were defining Jews by criteria derived directly from the Nuremberg Laws." Poland's "international reputation [was] once again—and for many years to come—inextricably associated with the victimization of its Jewish minority."[6]

In Eastern Europe, postwar authorities took care to label the Second World War an antifascist crusade—downplaying the racist character of Nazi brutality. At Auschwitz—a few kilometers from Kraków—where it was not possible to deny or minimize what had taken place, the evidence was misrepresented. "Although 93 percent of the estimated 1.5 million people murdered at Auschwitz were Jews, the museum established under the post-war Communist regime listed the victims only by nationality: Polish, Hungarian, German, etc. Polish schoolchildren were indeed paraded past the shocking photos; they were shown the heaps of shoes, hair and eyeglasses. But they were not told that most of it belonged to Jews."[7]

Timothy Snyder's portrayal of the occupied populations of Eastern Europe as victimized by two totalitarian powers echoed narratives that found favor in Hungary and Poland. With claims that their compatriots had been blameless, leaders in these two countries managed to avoid an honest reckoning with the wartime treatment of Jews. What is striking is how, along with their evasion of inconvenient truths, they trafficked in the old canards of anti-Semitism.

I. Denying Hungary's Past

Anti-Semitism was nothing new in interwar Hungary. In 1920, after the collapse of a short-lived Bolshevik regime and the consolidation of a semi-autocracy under Admiral Miklós Horthy, the so-called *numerus clausus* law, a law restricting the number of Jews admitted to institutions of higher education, was passed. It was the first piece of anti-Jewish legislation in interwar Europe. Though the law's most bigoted elements were canceled in 1928, this elimination did not decisively break the pattern of exclusion, and ten years later, the return of the *numerus clausus* provoked no surprise, let alone protest. Anti-Semitism, on the part of the public and politicians alike, grew apace, prompting a long list of restrictions: on Jews in business and the professions, on marriages and extramarital sex between Jews and non-Jews. In the course of almost two decades, people "had become accustomed to the idea that Jews may and can be singled out for … discriminatory legislation."[8]

During those same years, the main goal of Hungarian foreign policy had been revising the country's borders with its neighbors, Czechoslovakia, Rumania, and Yugoslavia. By the Treaty of Trianon, signed in 1920, Hungary was shorn of almost three-quarters of its territory and two-thirds of its inhabitants. The wish to reincorporate the areas that before 1918 had been under Hungarian administration provided the impetus for Hungary's alignment with Fascist Italy and Nazi Germany. And that alignment paid off. In 1938, the southern strip of Slovakia and in the spring of 1939, the Carpathian Ukraine, Slovakia's easternmost province, were handed over to Hungary; in the summer of 1940, Hungary seized northern Transylvania from Rumania and the Délvidék from Yugoslavia. This expansion almost doubled the Jewish population of Hungary.

Even before German troops entered Hungary on March 19, 1944, Hungarian Jews had suffered more than 60,000 casualties. Once Hungary joined Germany in the war against the Soviet Union in June 1941, Jewish men were conscripted into forced labor units. Roughly 40,000 of them perished. Then in July and August 1941, the Hungarian police and gendarmerie shoved between 16,000 and 18,000 "alien Jews"—those arbitrarily identified as not having Hungarian citizenship—into German-occupied Ukraine where, together with some 6,000 local Jews, they were murdered by the SS.[9] This *Aktion* constituted the first five-figure massacre of the Second World War. Next, in January and February 1942, Hungarian military units rounded up and killed close to a 1,000 Jews in Serbia. With the German occupation of Hungary—aimed at squashing any thought Horthy might have had of signing an armistice with the Allies—all Hungarian Jews were now within reach of the Nazis.[10]

When the Wehrmacht entered Hungary, Horthy stayed put and ordered the army not to resist. His decision to continue as head of state played into the hands of the Nazis who were eager to maintain a façade of Hungarian sovereignty—the better to maximize German exploitation of Hungary's economic and military resources, and the better to implement the Final Solution. To that end a special commando squad of around 150 to 200 men, organized under the immediate command of Adolf Eichmann, accompanied the German troops. It was in Hungary that Eichmann, finally, had the chance to test his effectiveness in the field.

And he was able to proceed with lightning speed—owing to the enthusiastic assistance of the Hungarian government. Within days of Eichmann's arrival, it adopted a framework for the isolation and expropriation of Jews. An initial decree required Jews to wear the Star of David, thus separating them from the Christian population; a second, addressed in confidence to the leading officials of the gendarmerie, police, and state administration, called for ghettoization and deportation. The techniques were basically the same throughout the country: Jewish leaders in each community were ordered to provide lists of all Jews along with their addresses. In hamlets, villages, and smaller towns, the police acted in concert with local civil servants. After a few weeks, the ghettoized were transferred to deportation centers, usually in county seats. Each day three or four trains were scheduled to depart, with each train carrying approximately 3,000 Jews. Throughout the entire process, "the Hungarian gendarmerie treated its victims with the utmost brutality."[11] Physical abuse, theft, and torture were the order of the day. On July 15, Edmund Veesenmayer, Hitler's plenipotentiary in Budapest, reported back to Berlin that 437,402 Jews had reached their destination—Auschwitz-Birkenau. Of these roughly 25 percent were selected for labor; the rest were murdered on arrival.[12]

Because the Red Army was fast approaching, instructions stipulated that Hungary be combed of Jews from East to West. Thus Budapest Jews were saved for last. On July 7, Horthy—having been deluged with protests from neutral countries, from the Vatican, and from the Allies, who drove home their disapproval by an unusually heavy air raid on Budapest—ordered the deportations to stop. Without Horthy's consent and the collaboration of Hungarian authorities, Eichmann could not continue with any large-scale operations.

This state of relative calm lasted until October 15. With the Red Army no more than a hundred miles from the capital, the Germans forced Horthy to resign and to transfer power to Ferenc Szálasi, leader of the Hungarian version of the Nazis, the Arrow Cross Party. Terror was unleashed against Jews in Budapest; deportations resumed as well. The Arrow Cross regime herded—mostly on foot—a total of 50,000 people to the country's western border or to the Reich. Again protests by neutral countries had a telling effect. Szálasi gradually stopped the death marches and his government began organizing ghettos instead. Liberation came on the heels of the Red Army in January 1945.

The story of what happened to Hungarian Jews is made clear in Budapest's Holocaust Memorial Center. This modern complex, which opened in 2004 (with a beautifully restored synagogue as its centerpiece), serves as a monument to the murder victims, a museum of the Hungarian Holocaust, a space for temporary exhibits, and a research and documentation center. The permanent exhibit shows just how pervasive anti-Semitism was in Hungary long before the Second World War. In every room there are text panels, interactive touch screens, and film clips; there are numerous audio points that zoom in on an individual or a single family, following their horrific experiences over the years. There is no whitewashing of the role Hungarians played in the persecution and deportation of the Jews.

* * * * * * * * * * * *

The Holocaust Memorial Center is tucked away and has relatively few visitors. In contrast the House of Terror is hugely popular, with tourists queuing around the block. Located at 60 Andrássy Avenue, the museum occupies a building with a complex and controversial past. It was here that the Arrow Cross had their headquarters and interrogated and tortured their opponents. And in the postwar period, it was here that the Communist secret police—the ÁVH—had their headquarters and interrogated and tortured their opponents. The House of Terror, according to the museum's brochure, was thus "witness to two shameful and tragic periods in Hungary's 20th century history."

Only two rooms in the House of Terror are devoted to giving an account of the Fascist era; seventeen outline in great detail the brutality of the Communist regime. The exhibition starts with the story of "double occupation."

> From the mid-thirties onward, Hungary found herself in the crossfire of the increasingly more aggressive Nazi Germany and the Soviet Union .... Allied with one another and subsequently locked in a life-and-death battle, the two totalitarian dictatorships strived for a new order that had no place for an independent Hungary. After the outbreak of World War II, Hungary made desperate attempts to maintain her albeit limited elbow room and to avert the worst scenario: German occupation. It was a great achievement that this could be averted for the first several years of the war, but on March 19th 1944, German forces occupied the country ....
>
> On August 27th 1944, Soviet troops crossed the Hungarian border. The country became the theatre of war in a clash between the two super powers. The short, but disastrous Nazi occupation was followed by Soviet rule, which established itself for a long duration. Hungary's sovereignty was lost on March 19th 1944, and occupying forces were stationed in the country for over four decades.[13]

A small space, the threshold between the Nazi and Communist versions of terror, is dedicated to "Changing Clothes." The flyer explains:

> In the 1939 parliamentary elections, the Arrow Cross became the second largest party with more than 300,000 members. The Hungarian national socialists were

supported by an electorate numbering close to a million. They received one in every three votes in the working class districts of Budapest.

The Communist party, operating illegally since 1919, consisted of only a few hundred members in the period preceding Soviet occupation .... [I]n the wake of the Red Army, the Communist Party of Hungary began to reorganize .... [T]here was a rush to join ... by certain elements that ... [to quote the General Secretary of the Hungarian Communist Party] "had been to a greater or lesser degree influenced by the counter-revolution and the corrupting effect of fascism."

Two uniforms, those of the Arrow Cross and the Communist secret police, rotate in the middle of the space. They "symbolize the continuity of the dictatorships." A "video clip depicts how an entire society was forced to become 'turncoats,' i.e. to switch alliances."[14]

This history of Hungary from 1944 to 1989 subsumes the Holocaust within a monolithic account of Hungarian victimhood. Both Jews and non-Jews alike are presented as victims of totalitarianism, Jews as victims of Nazi Germany and the native exponent of the foreign doctrine of fascism, the Arrow Cross, and non-Jews as victims of the Communist Soviet Union and their ÁVH henchmen. The specificity of the Holocaust is thus discounted.

* * * * * * * * * * * *

The last room in the House of Terror is labeled "Farewell." On one side of the door, the visitor can watch a video of the 1989 reburial of Imre Nagy, the executed hero of Hungary's 1956 anti-Soviet revolt. Here is Viktor Orbán (prime minister of Hungary in the year 2002) "as a young radical, anti-Communist, liberal, new-age politician" demanding the withdrawal of Soviet troops from Hungary. And on the other side, the final "image of the memorial is the opening ceremony of the House of Terror on February 24, 2002, ... less than six weeks before the next Hungarian general election."[15] Orbán did not win that election. Eight years later, he returned to power and set about remolding democracy and rewriting history.

In 1989, when Soviet power collapsed, Orbán was a law student at István Bibó College, an elite institution in Budapest. His daring speeches at anti-communist demonstrations sweeping Hungary made him a leading light of Fidesz, then a liberal student movement. A year later, he entered parliament and in 1998, he became prime minister. His surprise defeat in 2002 accelerated Fidesz's growing shift away from liberalism. In 2010, a wave of anger at the Socialist-led government allowed Fidesz to win a two-thirds majority in parliament with just 53 percent of the vote.

Orbán did not campaign on a promise to dismantle the rule of law. He presented his party as belonging to the mainstream. Once in office, it quickly set about using its super-majority to change the constitution, to align the executive, legislative, and judicial powers of the state. These branches would buttress each other and Fidesz, sometimes unobtrusively, sometimes blatantly. There would be elections, more or less free though not fair, but the real backbone of the Western political system, checks and balances, limits on the action of government, would be gone. Orbán openly admitted that he was building what he called an "illiberal democracy"—and he was proud of it.

One of the first things that Fidesz did after winning a parliamentary super-majority in 2010 was to rewrite the constitution. Adopted on April 25, 2011, the preamble reads:

> We date the restoration of our country's self-determination, lost on the nineteenth day of March 1944, from the second day of May 1990, when the first freely elected organ of popular representation was formed. We shall consider this date to be the beginning of our country's new democracy and constitutional order.

In this fashion, the Orbán government claimed that Hungary had lost its sovereignty at the beginning of the German occupation and that, as a victim itself, it was not responsible for the subsequent destruction of Hungarian Jews. Orbán thus erased the fact that the German occupiers were well received by most Hungarians, civilians and military alike, that the Horthy-appointed government placed the instruments of state power at the disposal of those in charge of the Final Solution, and that Horthy continued to represent the sovereignty of the nation as head of state.

A few days after Fidesz's victory in 2014, again winning a super-majority in parliament, but, this time, with less than half the popular vote, construction workers put the finishing touches on a new addition to Freedom Square. Standing in the middle of a broken colonnade, an innocent-looking Archangel Gabriel holds a sphere with a double cross (a symbol of Hungarian sovereignty). Overhead, a black eagle, crafted to resemble the one on the German coat of arms, dives toward him, its talons poised to strike. The year 1944 is attached to the eagle's ankle. "In Memory of the Victims of the German Occupation" reads the inscription at the base of the monument. The initial plans for the memorial had drawn protests from Jewish organizations leading Orbán to postpone work on it until after the election. Then, in the dead of night, the Hungarian government slipped the angel and the eagle into the square.

* * * * * * * * * * *

The preamble to the constitution, with its insistence on the continuity between the Hungarian state of the Horthy era and the Hungarian state of the post-Communist period, signaled an acceleration of the campaign to rehabilitate Horthy, a campaign that began not long after the departure of the last Soviet troops. Streets, parks, and public squares were renamed in his honor. In 2013, in the heart of Budapest, a bust was unveiled on the grounds of the Hungarian Reformed Church. The Calvinist minister blessed it; then an MP from the extreme-right Jobbik party "addressed the congregation, declaring Horthy to be 'the greatest statesman of the 20th century.'"[16] This growing Horthy cult may have been promoted by Jobbik, but Fidesz did not try to stop it—it meshed too well with Orbán's nationalist priorities.

The irredentism dominating the official politics and discourse during the Horthy years was followed by long, deep silence imposed by the Communists. After 1989, that changed. Talk about past grievances, particularly the Treaty of Trianon, became possible, indeed a staple on the right. Those who failed to join in the condemnation of Trianon were considered beyond the pale. Orbán, both in opposition and in power, insisted that "the socialists have always attacked the nation both in the past and in the present," and that "the liberals represent an alien-hearted component of the country's population." Neither "belong to the authentic national political community."[17]

Talk about Trianon turned out not to be mere talk. In 2011, Orbán granted voting rights to some 2 million ethnic Hungarians who were citizens of neighboring Rumania, Slovakia, Serbia, and Ukraine, and who overwhelmingly plump for Fidesz. They are allowed to vote by mail. The roughly 350,000 Hungarian citizens living in the West are much less likely to support the party. They have to vote in person at embassies or consulates. Despite these electoral advantages—add in the gerrymandering of single-member districts—Fidesz could not maintain its dominant position, if it were not popular. Its ethnic nationalism has proved an effective strategy.[18]

So too has Orbán's Christian revival. Every summer he gives a speech in Transylvania, "to an enclave of ethnic Hungarians who were stranded in Rumania after the Treaty of Trianon. Orbán uses the occasion as a kind of state-of-the-union address." It was here, in 2014, that he broadcast his claim "to be constructing in Hungary ... an illiberal state, a non-liberal state." Four years later, Orbán refined his idea. "There is an alternative to liberal democracy; it is called Christian democracy .... And we must show that the liberal élite can be replaced by a Christian-democratic élite." Orbán provided some clarification. "Liberal democracy is in favor of multiculturalism, while Christian democracy gives priority to Christian culture .... Liberal democracy is pro-immigration, while Christian democracy is anti-immigration."[19]

In the Horthy era, Hungarians, across the political spectrum, had not only grieved over their lost territories; they had also embraced the ideology of Christian nationalism, a belief that Hungary would be renewed if it restored "Christian values" to national life.[20] Orbán sounded similar themes. To distinguish the current regime both from its avowedly secular communist predecessor and from the liberal atheistic West, he repurposed Christianity. Mixing religion and nationalism has turned out to be a toxic brew: in recalling Europe's Christian roots, Orbán has brought anti-Semitism and Islamophobia into alignment.

* * * * * * * * * * *

In January 2015, two French brothers of Algerian parentage killed twelve people in an attack on the satirical weekly *Charlie Hebdo*. Orbán went to Paris to attend a huge rally for national unity. He took the occasion to announce zero tolerance for immigrants:

> As long as I am prime minister and as long as this government is in power, we will not allow Hungary to become the destination of immigrants .... We do not want to see in our midst any minorities whose cultural background differs from our own. We want to keep Hungary for Hungarians.

Orbán's declaration inaugurated a major propaganda campaign, with huge posters and signs all over the country ostensibly aimed at foreign migrants: "'If you come to Hungary, you must respect Hungarian culture!' But ... the billboards and the government-sponsored advertisements were in Hungarian."[21] No migrant, heading to Western Europe, who ended up in Hungary would have understood them.

Until 2015, Hungary received around 3,000 asylum requests a year. That year, hundreds of thousands of people, mostly from Iraq, Syria, and Afghanistan, traveled from Turkey through Bulgaria to Serbia and Croatia, where they attempted to cross the Hungarian border into the EU. Many wanted to reach

Germany, where Chancellor Angela Merkel, declaring, "We can do this," welcomed a million refugees. That summer, Orbán's government began to construct a fence along Hungary's border with Serbia and Croatia, essentially halting immigration to Hungary. Orbán's transparent and crude offensive to rouse public opinion against foreign refugees outflanked the far-right Jobbik, while the divided and disheartened left retreated in disarray. It was a great public relations success for his regime.

Orban's public enemy number one has been the Hungarian-born American investor George Soros. The media empires directly and indirectly controlled by Fidesz made "a bogeyman out of a Holocaust survivor who, through his Open Society Foundation … [had] spent $12 billion to promote liberal democracy, social justice and human rights."[22] They portrayed him as *the* person responsible for the flood of refugees. "Billboards paid for by Fidesz showed a Photoshopped image of a grinning Soros, his arms around the shoulders of opposition politicians, who clutched garden shears and peered expectantly through a hole they'd cut in the border fence …. Members of Fidesz categorically … [denied] that their campaign against Soros … [was] anti-Semitic. But, Orbán said, 'we must fight against an opponent who is different from us …. They do not fight directly, but by stealth. They are not honorable, but unprincipled. They are not national, but international. They do not believe in work, but speculate with money. They have no homeland, but feel that the whole world is theirs.'"[23] In Orbán's telling, Hungary is locked in a fight with Soros for nothing less than its national existence.

Speaking in 2016, Soros, for his part, saw Orbán as exploiting a mix of ethnic and religious nationalism:

> And Orbán is not alone. The leader of the newly elected ruling party in Poland, Jarosław Kaczyński, is taking a similar approach …. [H]e is a canny politician and he chose migration as the central issue of his campaign. Poland is one of the most ethnically and religiously homogenous countries in Europe. A Muslim immigrant in Catholic Poland is the embodiment of the Other. Kaczyński was successful in painting him as the devil.[24]

II. Defending Poland's Honor

Kaczyński had been among the leaders of the Solidarity movement who negotiated Poland's bloodless transition to democracy in 1989. The coalition that had emerged split in 2001, into the mainstream Civic Platform and the anti-elitist Law and Justice. In 2005, Law and Justice took a quarter of the vote, enough for a plurality in parliament. But its unruly alliance with two other anti-establishment parties lasted only two years. Thereafter the centrist Civic Platform held sway. By 2015, it had grown complacent and its charismatic leader, Donald Tusk, had stepped down as prime minister to become president of the European Council, leaving his party rudderless. Law and Justice swept into power winning an unprecedented absolute majority. Kaczyński, though he held no office other than MP, acted as Poland's de facto leader. With control of parliament and a sympathetic president, his party began pushing Poland toward the sort of "illiberal democracy" Orbán had created in Hungary. It set about dismantling the institutional framework of parliamentary democracy: it stacked the courts, skewed public media, and stuffed the bureaucracy with its supporters.[25]

In 2015, the party won by latching onto the refugee crisis. Aided by images of migrants pouring into Europe—none of whom came near to Poland—it exploited fears of a Muslim invasion. Until then "Poles had never given much thought to Islam beyond occasionally a sense of historical pride that a Polish king, Jan Sobieski, defeated the Turks in a 17th century battle near Vienna, thus saving Christian Europe from the infidels." This fit with a recurrent theme in Polish national mythology: "Poland as a rampart of Christianity, the Christ of Nations. Poland, according to this trope, has repeatedly, and heroically, suffered for the sake of others, especially the rest of Christian Europe."[26] And when, in 2019, Kaczyński kicked off a new—and successful—campaign season, he proclaimed that "Christianity is part of our national identity. The [Catholic] church was and is a preacher and possessor of the only system of values fully known in Poland …. Besides the church there is only nihilism."[27]

The rise of Law and Justice had been fueled by anger over the publication in Poland, in 2000, of Jan Gross's *Neighbors*, a history of the Polish-perpetrated mass murder of Jews in Jedwabne on July 10, 1941. The town had been occupied by the Soviets and then fell to the Germans at the start of Operation Barbarossa. In Jedwabne, neighbors turned out to be killers and Polish citizens—traditionally seen as both heroic resisters and innocent victims—turned out to be tools of Nazi genocidal policy. Gross, a Polish-born American academic, was denounced for defaming Poland.

* * * * * * * * * * *

The appearance of *Neighbors*, Gross commented, produced "a long and, perhaps, the most complex confrontation with collective memory, and the need to revise it, that the Poles had ever faced. Radio and television programs, newspaper articles and interviews, essays in professional journals ... numbered in the thousands. The story reached into every nook and cranny of ... Polish society."[28] In September 2000, the Institute of National Remembrance announced that it was launching its own inquiry. At the same time, Anna Bikont, a journalist for the *Gazeta Wyborcza*, a leading liberal newspaper, took unpaid leave to go to Jedwabne to try to lay bare the facts and to find out what had "happened to the memory of those events over the last sixty years."[29]

In the final chapter of her book, *The Crime and the Silence*, Bikont reported on a conversation she had had with Radosław Ignatiew, the prosecutor who had conducted the investigation for the Institute of National Remembrance.

> *When did you first realize that the story Gross told had really happened?*
> That wasn't the goal of my investigation. I wasn't concerned with whether Gross's book was good or bad, true or false ....
> *All right .... So let's reconstruct what can be known.*
> From the early hours of the morning, Jews were driven from their homes into the market square. They were ordered to pull up grass from between the paving stones. The residents of Jedwabne and its surroundings were armed with sticks, crow bars, and other weapons. A large group of men were forced to smash the Lenin monument, which was in the little square off the market. Around noon they were ordered to carry a piece of the smashed monument to the market square, and then to the barn a few hundred meters away. They carried it on two wooden poles. The rabbi was among them. Victims were killed and their bodies were thrown into a grave dug inside the barn. Pieces of the Lenin monument were flung on top of the corpses. The grave was probably not covered because at the time of the exhumation they found burn marks on some of the pieces of the monument. The second, larger group of Jews was brought to the market square later. It included women, children, old people. They were led to the thatched wooden barn. The building had gas thrown on it from the former Soviet storehouse in Jedwabne ....
> *Does that mean that the people in the second group saw the massacred bodies of their fathers, brothers, and sons before meeting their own deaths?*
> It is possible.
> *Did you ascertain what the last walk of the Jews of Jedwabne was like?*
> Quotidian objects were found with the remains, like a box with shoemaker's nails, tailor's thimbles, spoons, gold coins, and a surprising number of keys: to gates, houses, padlocks, cabinets. As if they had the illusory hope that they were setting off on a path from which they would return one day.[30]

Turning to the question of numbers—how many were murdered—Ignatiew was confident that the figure of 1,600 was improbable. That figure had been inscribed on a stone marking the place of execution and had been cited by Gross.[31]

> I asked all the witnesses about it and one of them had a convincing answer: "After the war I served in a unit, we had a roll call of about five or six hundred soldiers—and I associate that visually with the number of Jews I saw when they were led out of the market." There were forty or fifty in the group carrying fragments of the Lenin monument; in the second group—several hundred, we can say no fewer than three hundred. That is the approximate number of victims found in the two open graves .... We probably didn't find all the places where victims were buried. But even with earlier killings in others places, it is hard to imagine there were more people killed separately than were burned later in the barn.[32]

The stone had also been inscribed with the preferred Polish account of the massacre—that the "Gestapo and Hitler's Police" had been the guilty parties. Bikont questioned Ignatiew about its accuracy.

> [C]an we determine whether the Germans put forward the idea "to clean up the Jews ..." or merely accepted and supported the tendencies of the locals, expressed by the town authorities? ...
>
> It is not possible that ... the crime in Jedwabne ... happened without German acceptance. You have to keep in mind that Jedwabne was just behind the front line, in an area under German administration. In the event of unexpected ... unrest in the town, the occupation forces would have reacted immediately. The presence, even passive of German policemen ... as well as other uniformed Germans—if we accept that they were there—is in the eye of the law equivalent to permission to commit the crime ....
>
> Many witnesses say that the locals who drove the Jews into the square were accompanied by some uniformed Germans, apart from those from the police station. It was certainly a small group, not a powerful unit. The Germans had too many towns to guard .... We have German reports of that time that express alarm: "We don't have anyone to man the posts." ...
>
> *In other words, the Germans' role was to egg on the local population?*
>
> What does egging on mean? If there hadn't been the conditions for the perpetration of a crime like that, no amount of egging on would have had any effect. ... It seems to me that the Germans took advantage of the strong anti-Semitic feeling that already existed [in Jedwabne] ....
>
> I can state that the perpetrators of the atrocity were Polish residents of Jedwabne and its surroundings, at least forty men. There is no proof that the

townspeople in general were the perpetrators .... To claim that there was a company of Germans in Jedwabne is as implausible as maintaining that the whole town went crazy.

A few hundred burned in the barn, forty killers—that's a lot fewer than Gross wrote.[33]

Early in her search, Bikont had attended a colloquium held at the Polish Academy of Sciences convened to discuss *Neighbors*. After several people pointed out "scholarly shortcomings" in the book, Marek Edelman, the last surviving leader of the Warsaw Ghetto Uprising, approached the microphone.

> Everybody here would like to find some proof that Gross is a shoddy historian, that he made a mistake and Mr. So-and-So was killed earlier and Mrs. Such-and-Such later. But that's not what this is about .... Jedwabne was not the first case, nor was it an isolated one. In Poland at that time the mood was ripe for killing Jews.[34]

* * * * * * * * * * *

As the sixtieth anniversary of the massacre drew near, a commemorative ceremony was planned in Jedwabne. Would, Bikont wondered, the Church participate? The Primate, Cardinal Józef Glemp, made clear that it would not. He announced that, instead, church dignitaries would gather in Warsaw on May 27.

> The Episcopal Convention will pray—he stressed—not only for the Jewish victims in Jedwabne but also "for the evil visited upon Polish citizens of the Catholic faith, in which Poles of the Jewish faith took part .... The Poles," the primate continued, "were also wronged ... suffered from evil perpetrated by Jews, including the period when Communism was introduced in Poland. I expect the Jewish side to make a reckoning with its conscience and bring itself to apologize to the Poles for these crimes."

Days later, he gave what Bikont considered "a shocking interview."

> The primate says that for a long time now the Church has been subjected to a smear campaign aimed at making it apologize for crimes against Jews; Gross's book was clearly written on commission and the massacre in Jedwabne had no religious subtext whatsoever. After which he pulls out a full array of anti-Semitic clichés including pearls like this: "The Jews are smarter and knew how to exploit the Poles," and "Jews were disliked for their strange folklore." ... At the end, the primate says, "anti-Semitism doesn't exist; however, anti-Polishness does."[35]

Father (Stanisław) Musiał, a Kraków Jesuit, struck a very different note.

> In connection with the tragedy of Jedwabne I have for months been hearing and reading protests, some by my theologian colleagues, against asking for forgiveness .... Let us not forget, however, that Jewish neighbors were murdered not by Methodists or Mormons, but by Polish Catholics .... These people probably went to mass on Sunday. It was celebrated by a priest who on [the previous] Thursday had not saved the Jews and their tormentors—his parishioners—from the crime.[36]

No one, Bikont commented, pointed "to anti-Semitism as a sin of the Polish Church as clearly as Father Musiał." And because of it, he suffered "various kinds of trouble and chicanery from church authorities."[37]

At the ceremony, President Aleksander Kwaśniewski issued a formal apology "in my own name and in the name of those Poles whose consciences are shattered by that crime; in the name of those who believe that one cannot be proud of the glory of Polish history without feeling, at the same time, pain and shame for the evil done by Poles to others."[38] He did not speak for the majority of his constituents: "in a poll conducted around the same time, 60 percent of the respondents opposed offering any apology for the pogrom," and almost all of Jedwabne's residents boycotted the proceedings.[39]

A debate had broken out earlier over the wording of a new monument to replace the one that held the Gestapo responsible for the crime. The new inscription reads:

> *In memory of the Jews of Jedwabne and surroundings, men, women, children, fellow stewards of this land, murdered and burned alive in this place on July 10, 1941. A warning to posterity that the sin of hatred incited by German Nazism should never again turn the residents of this land against one another.*

Bikont was appalled: it left out "who committed the atrocity."[40]

* * * * * * * * * * * *

In late 2012, the Polish film *Aftermath* (*Pokłosie*) was released, reigniting the controversy that had surrounded the publication of *Neighbors*. The movie, declared its director, Władysław Pasikowski, "isn't an adaptation of the book ... , but the film did grow out of it, since it was the source of my knowledge and shame."[41]

Aftermath drew intense criticism from Polish nationalists. Over the following months, it so riled the Polish right wing that it was banned from some local cinemas, while its leading actor, Maciej Stuhr, received death threats. A cover on Poland's largest weekly, *Wprost*, framed his image in a Jewish star with the headline, "Maciej Stuhr Lynched and Asking for It." Inside, the article called Stuhr "a walking symbol of simplifying and manipulating history for the sake of commercial success."[42] Dariusz Jabłonski, one of the film's producers, commented, "We all knew we were dealing with a subject that was still very much a taboo."[43]

Set around 2000, at the time of the Jedwabne debate, in the same impoverished region of northeast Poland, the movie tells the story of Franciszek Kalina (Ireneusz Czop), a Pole living in Chicago, who begrudgingly returns to his native village. Here his brother Józef (Stuhr) maintains the family farm. Nothing has changed in the village; Józef has. He spends his nights uncovering tombstones that were stripped from the Jewish cemetery and used for a roadbed (a common practice in Poland both during and after the war). He plants them firmly into an ad hoc graveyard he has created in one of his fields. Having taught himself how to read the Hebrew inscriptions, he painstakingly cleans and restores the markers. When asked why he is consumed by this project, all he can say is, "They were human beings."

For his part, Franciszek is casually anti-Semitic: he complains that in Chicago, Jews have "cornered" the construction business—"they sure don't let a Pole make an honest buck over there." Yet it is he who takes the lead in bringing the past to light. The shift comes when Józef, needing a loan, is unable to prove that he has a clear title to his property. Sifting through old records, Franciszek learns that his father had seized land that belonged to murdered Jews. Asking hard questions of old people who had lived through the war, then digging up the remains of the dead, he learns that the Jews of the village—twenty-six families—had been burned alive in what had been his family's home, and that his father, along with a neighbor, had lighted the blaze.

In their attempt to investigate the past, the brothers are demonized and called Jewish slurs. Franciszek is shadowed and treated with suspicion; Józef is harassed and beaten up. A rock is thrown through a window of the farmhouse and anti-Semitic graffiti is painted on the walls. Józef's dog is beheaded. One night his fields are set on fire, and no one will help put out the flames. This unblinking representation of the brutality directed at the Kalina brothers—the hatred of the villagers, their menacing scowls, grunts of contempt—contributes to the film's power.

Still, the ending comes as a shock. Now aware of their father's role in the murder of the Jews, Józef wants to do nothing further. Franciszek adopts the opposite line: he wants to speak out. They have a terrible fight. Franciszek leaves, but his bus is stopped. He returns to find Józef beaten, stabbed, lynched, and nailed high on the inside of the barn door. His arms are outstretched, his wrists and feet held by wooden cleats. The assembled villagers look on, stone-faced.

The brothers had threatened to reveal not the truth, but the cover-up of the truth. The elderly villagers knew full well what had happened to the Jews and had covered it up. And this conspiracy of silence had continued into the next generations.

III. Coda

In 1988, Harvard law professor Alan Dershowitz issued a warning:

> I want to make a strong pitch for why courts and governments should never be allowed to be the arbiters of truth; should never be allowed to be arbiters of whether a particular historical event occurred or didn't occur. I am categorically opposed to any court, any school board, any governmental agent taking judicial notice of any historical event, even one I know ... occurred, like the Holocaust .... Because, inevitably, if a government can say the Holocaust occurred, then another government somewhere, sometime, can say it didn't occur.[44]

In the following years, numerous nations sought to turn Holocaust denial into a criminal offense. In France, in 1990, the Gayssot law, named after the French communist legislator who drafted it, made it a crime to deny or minimize the Holocaust. In France, repugnant speech isn't just repugnant; it is illegal. Four years later, Germany amended its criminal code to include the denial and trivialization of the Nazi genocide as a form of racial incitement. In effect, the German law "demands that no one deny the state's monstrous past."[45]

In 2016, Law and Justice introduced a bill known as the "Polish-death-camps amendment." It included a sentence of up to three years in prison for any false claim that "the Polish Nation or the Republic of Poland is responsible or co-responsible for Nazi crimes committed by the Third Reich."[46] The amendment was meant to put an end to the phrase "Polish death camps" which many Poles felt blamed the country for atrocities that took place on Polish soil. In the two years after the change was proposed, it made its way through the legislative process despite warnings from parliamentary committees that its wording was poor and essentially unenforceable. On January 26, 2018, the day before International Holocaust Remembrance Day, the bill cleared the Polish parliament. Fearful that

President Andrzej Duda would veto it, a bunch of thugs demonstrated outside the presidential palace urging him to "tear off his yarmulke" (he is not Jewish).[47] He signed.

To Law and Justice, the real purpose of the act was never Poland's international image. (Following widespread protests, at home and abroad, the amendment was subsequently itself amended, replacing criminal with civil penalties.) In a sharp break with all previous democratic governments of right, left, and center, going back to 1989, Law and Justice did not care—or did not care very much—how isolated the country became. On the contrary, foreign criticism offered another chance to solidify the support of "patriots" who opposed the "slander" of the country versus "traitors" who did not. The international reaction to the law simply cemented the government's narrative that it alone could be relied upon to defend the honor of the Polish nation.

Conclusion

The perversion of Holocaust memory—the refusal to reckon with their compatriots active contribution to the Nazi project of extermination—has been central to the appeal of governments in Hungary and Poland. In Western Europe, a similar disposition can be found on the far right. The reactionary Alternative für Deutschland, or AfD, which entered the Bundestag for the first time in 2017 and became the third-largest party, railed against Germany's remembrance culture, calling it a national "guilt cult." In a speech in 2018, Alexander Gaulaud, a party leader, referred to the Nazi period as "only a bird poop in over 1,000 years of successful German history."[1] Two decades earlier, the Front National had already become a firmly established fixture in the French political landscape. Its leader, Jean-Marie Le Pen, claimed that the gas chambers were merely "a minor point in the history of World War II."[2] His daughter and political heir, Marine Le Pen, tried to cleanse the Front National—now renamed the Rassemblement National—of its anti-Semitic reputation. That effort came undone when she claimed that France was not responsible for the Vél d'Hiv roundup in 1942. Vichy, she tried to explain, was not France. France, she continued, "has been mistreated, in people's minds, for years."[3]

A recurring theme: victimhood. In Hungary, Viktor Orbán and his cronies present their country as doubly victimized, first by Germany, and then by the Soviet Union. In Poland, Law and Justice points to eastern Poland as a victim three times over: of Soviet troops in 1939, of German armies in 1941, and then at war's end of the Soviet Union once again. And Holocaust pedagogy, made concrete in Berlin's Memorial to the Murdered Jews of Europe—a "monument of shame," claimed the AfD—amounts, so say a number of Germans, among others, to a kind of national defamation. Let the Nazis—or the Western Allies—or the Soviets—stand as the designated villains. Spare the German people, and the Hungarians, and the Poles, and the French for that matter.

Victimhood shades readily into paranoia. At base, far-right governments and far-right parties "have one thing in common: their belief that some form of pure, integral community—nation, race, religion—is under threat. The brilliance of their message lies in its ability to portray demographic majorities as embattled minorities. In this weird alchemy of essentialist politics a Syrian grocer or a Tunisian cab driver becomes an agent of cosmic doom."[4]

And it shades into conspiracy thinking as well. Writing about mid-century America, Richard Hofstadter pointed to "the central preconception of the paranoid style—the existence of a vast, insidious, preternaturally effective international conspiratorial network designed to perpetrate acts of the most fiendish character …. The paranoid spokesman sees the fate of this conspiracy in apocalyptic terms—he traffics in the birth and death of whole worlds, whole political orders, whole systems of human values. He is always manning the barricades of civilization."[5]

A case in point: *le grand remplacement*—the great replacement. Renaud Camus made this the title of his alarmist book which appeared in 2012. Native white Europeans, he argued, "are being reverse colonized by black and brown immigrants, who are flooding the continent in what amounts to an extinction-level event." All Western countries, he claimed, "are faced with varying degrees of 'ethnic and civilizational substitution.'" On August 11, 2017, a procession, led by Unite the Right, marched through the campus of the University of Virginia. "White supremacist protesters mashed together Nazi and Confederate iconography, while chanting variations of Camus's *grand remplacement* credo: 'You will not replace us'; 'Jews will not replace us.'"[6]

Why Jews? How could Jews—a very small minority in the United States—replace the white majority? Clearly numbers were not the issue. No, the demonstrators, who paraded with lighted tiki torches, were drawing on clichés of traditional anti-Semitism: Jewish wealth, organized Jewry, a Jewish conspiracy. The figure of "the Jew" turns out to be alive and kicking both in the United States and in Europe.

"Never again"—the mantra constantly recited in the wake of the Holocaust—is meant to serve as a tocsin, to alert one and all to the danger of repeating the past.[7] Holocaust remembrance is supposed to act as a bar not only to anti-Semitism but to ethnic nationalism more generally. What has now become clear is that this is wide of the mark: it misrepresents the impact of the present on the writing of history. Contemporary political battles can undo—can pervert—an understanding of the past that was hard won and once widely shared.

Notes

Introduction

1. Tony Judt, *Postwar: A History of Europe since 1945* (New York: Penguin, 2005), pp. 803–4. See also Omer Bartov, "Eastern Europe as the Site of Genocide," *Journal of Modern History* 80/3 (2008): 566.
2. Paul Hanebrink, *A Specter Haunting Europe: The Myth of Judeo-Bolshevism* (Cambridge, MA: Harvard University Press, 2018), p. 194.
3. See Bill Niven, *Facing the Nazi Past: United Germany and the Legacy of the Third Reich* (London: Routledge, 2001), p. 2.
4. See Judt, *Postwar*, p. 818, and Henry Rousso, *The Vichy Syndrome: History and Memory in France since 1944*, trans. Arthur Goldhammer (Cambridge, MA: Harvard University Press, 1991), p. 133.
5. See Saul Friedländer, *Nazi Germany and the Jews*, 2 vols. (New York: HarperCollins, 1997–2007).
6. See Judith M. Hughes, *The Holocaust and the Revival of Psychological History* (New York: Cambridge University Press, 2015), ch. 2.
7. See, for example, Monika Pronczuk and Marc Santora, "After a Neck-and-Neck Race for Polish President, Duda Wins a Second Term," *New York Times*, July 14, 2020.
8. For a recent—and hopeful—report on how migrants are faring in Germany, see Thomas Rogers, "Welcome to Germany," *New York Review of Books*, April 29, 2021.

Chapter 1

1. Éric Conan and Henry Rousso, *Vichy: An Ever-Present Past*, trans. Nathan Bracher (Hanover, NH: University Press of New England, 1998), p. 43. For the text of Chirac's speech, see ibid., pp. 39–42.
2. See Robert O. Paxton, "Finally France Confronts Its Nazi Shadow," *New York Times*, October 16, 1997.
3. Robert O. Paxton, *Vichy France: Old Guard and New Order, 1940–1944* (New York: Knopf, 1972).
4. Laurent Greilsamer, "Maurice Papon dans la prison du temps," *Le Monde*, October 9, 1997.

5 *Trial of the Major War Criminals before the International Military Tribunal, Nuremberg, November 14, 1945–October 1, 1946*, 42 vols. (Nuremberg: International Military Tribunal, 1947), 1: 11, quoted in Lawrence Douglas, *The Memory of Judgment: Making Law and History in the Trials of the Holocaust* (New Haven, CT: Yale University Press, 2001), pp. 46–7.

6 Elihu Lauterpacht, *Life of Hersch Lauterpacht* (Cambridge: Cambridge University Press, 2012), p. 274, quoted in Philippe Sands, *East West Street: On the Origins of "Genocide" and "Crimes Against Humanity"* (New York: Knopf, 2016), p. 115.

7 See Serge Klarsfeld, *The Children of Izieu: A Human Tragedy*, trans. Kenneth Jacobson (New York: H. Abrams, 1985).

8 See Beate Klarsfeld and Serge Klarsfeld, *Hunting the Truth: Memoirs of Beate and Serge Klarsfeld*, trans. Sam Taylor (New York: Farrar, Straus and Giroux, 2018).

9 See Annette Wieviorka, "France and Trials for Crimes against Humanity," in Austin Sarat, Lawrence Douglas, and Martha Merrill Umphrey, eds., *Lives in Law* (Ann Arbor: University of Michigan Press, 2002), pp. 215–31.

10 Douglas, *The Memory of Judgment*, p. 196.

11 See Richard J. Golsan, *Vichy's Afterlife: History and Counterhistory in Postwar France* (Lincoln: University of Nebraska Press, 2000), p. 89. For a fictional account of Touvier's years as a fugitive, see Brian Moore, *The Statement* (New York: Dutton, 1996).

12 The French legal procedure is very different from the American. Before being brought in front of a court, the accused is taken into custody and interviewed by an independent examining magistrate, who alone is empowered to conduct investigations (with the help of the Criminal Investigations Department). This phase of the preliminary investigation leads either to the charges being dismissed or to the case being sent on. Major felonies are referred to the Indicting Chamber of the Court of Appeals for a pretrial hearing. This court decides whether to approve the examining magistrate's recommendation, and if it does, the case is turned over to the Assize Court.

The Assize Court is responsible for trying the most serious crimes and is composed of a nine-member jury (drawn at random from the general population) and three magistrates. These twelve participate in the final deliberations and deliver a verdict.

In an assize trial, the accused, who is presumed innocent, is subjected to questioning throughout the trial and, since he or she is not required to be sworn in, has a legal right to lie. The witnesses can be summoned by the prosecuting attorney, plaintiffs, or the defense attorney. The witnesses testify without interruption, then the judge, prosecutor, plaintiff (if represented by a lawyer), and defense ask any further questions. The accused is always given the last word.

13 Wieviorka, "France and Trials for Crimes against Humanity," p. 222. In 1992, the penal code was revised to enlarge the notion of crimes against humanity beyond

what the High Court of Appeals had ruled. The restriction of acting on behalf of a state practicing a policy of ideological hegemony disappeared. See "Les crimes contre l'humanité dans le nouveau code pénal," *Le Monde*, April 24, 1994.
14 Conan and Rousso, *Vichy: An Ever-Present Past*, p. 91.
15 The role of the High Court is not to re-judge a case but to assess the judicial regularity of decisions that are submitted to it.
16 See Leila Sadat Wexler, "The Interpretation of the Nuremberg Principles by the French Court of Cassation: From Touvier to Barbie and Back Again," *The Columbia Journal of Transnational Law* 32 (1994): 289–380; Leila Sadat Wexler, "Reflections on the Trial of Vichy Collaborator Paul Touvier for Crimes against Humanity in France," *Law and Social Inquiry* 20 (Winter 1995): 191–221; Nancy Wood, "Crimes or Misdemeanors? Memory on Trial in Contemporary France," *French Cultural Studies* 5 (1994): 1–21.
17 Henry Rousso, "What Historians Will Retain from the Last Trial of the Purge," in Richard J. Golsan, ed., *Memory, the Holocaust, and French Justice: The Bousquet and Touvier Affairs*, trans. Lucy Golsan and Richard J Golsan (Hanover, NH: University Press of New England, 1996), p. 165.
18 See Tzvetan Todorov, "The Touvier Trial," in Golsan, *Memory, the Holocaust, and French Justice*, pp. 169–78.
19 See Leila Nadya Sadat, "The Legal Legacy of Maurice Papon," in Richard J. Golsan, ed., *The Papon Affair: Memory and Justice on Trial* (New York and London: Routledge, 2000), pp. 131–60.
20 Golsan, *Vichy's Afterlife*, p. 165; see also Bernard Violet, *Le dossier Papon* (Paris: Flammarion, 1997), pp. 51–90.
21 It has been commonplace, thanks to Jean-Luc Einaudi's *La bataille de Paris: 17 octobre 1961* (Paris: Seuil, 1991), to claim that 200 Algerians were killed in the police action. More recent work, in archives opened up as a result of the Papon trial, now suggests that the number of Algerians killed may have been closer to fifty. "Whatever the number, all serious studies of the repression have documented that the police were guilty of extreme brutality and murder, unleashing a wave of terror against Algerian demonstrators." William B. Cohen, "The Algerian War, the French State and Official Memory," *Historical Reflections/Réflexions Historiques* 28 (2002): 223n10. For a discussion of texts by anticolonial activists that addressed the October 17 massacre, see Michael Rothberg, *Multidirectional Memory: Remembering the Holocaust in the Age of Decolonization* (Stanford, CA: Stanford University Press, 2009), ch. 7.
22 Jim House and Neil MacMaster, "'Une Journée Portée Disparue': The Paris Massacre of 1961 and Memory," in Kenneth Mouré and Martin S. Alexander, eds., *Crisis and Renewal in France* (New York: Berghahn Books, 2008), pp. 271–2.
23 Ibid., p. 273.

24 See Éric Conan, *Le procès Papon: un journal d'audience* (Paris: Gallimard, 1998), p. 26.
25 *Le procès de Maurice Papon: compte rendu sténographique*, 2 vols. (Paris: Albin Michel, 1998), 1: 198. On this issue, Papon, as was his right, had the last word: see ibid., 1: 285–6.
26 For Einaudi's testimony, see ibid., 1: 225–44.
27 See ibid., 1: 230.
28 See Philippe Bernard, "Le tribunal correctionnel de Paris reconnaît l'extrême violence' de la repression du 17 octobre 1961," *Le Monde*, March 28, 1999.
29 "Pierre Vidal-Naquet, historien: 'Il se manifeste une gigantesque envie de vérité à propos de l'Algérie,'" *Le Monde*, November 27, 2000.
30 Frachra Gibbons, "François Hollande Tells the Truth—It Hurts Less than Lies," *Guardian*, October 19, 2012.
31 Françoise Fressoz, "Guerre d'Algérie: 'Macron est suffisamment vierge pour ouvrir l'inventaire,'" *Le Monde*, September 13, 2018.
32 Henry Rousso, author of *The Vichy Syndrome: History and Memory in France since 1944*, trans. Arthur Goldhammer (Cambridge, MA: Harvard University Press, 1991) and recognized as a major figure, was asked by the defense to testify and refused. See his explanation for his refusal: Henry Rousso, *The Haunting Past: History, Memory, and Justice in Contemporary France*, trans. Ralph Schoolcraft (Philadelphia: University of Pennsylvania Press, 2002). See also Donald Reid, "The Trial of Maurice Papon: History on Trial?" *French Politics and Society* 16 (1998): 62–79, and Richard J. Evans, "History, Memory and the Law: The Historian as Expert Witness," *History and Theory* 41 (2002): 326–45.
33 For Paxton's testimony, see *Le procès de Maurice Papon*, 1: 302–20. See also "Robert Paxton donne une accablante leçon d'histoire," *L'Humanité*, November 1, 1997.
34 See Vicki Caron, *Uneasy Asylum: France and the Jewish Refugee Crisis, 1933–1942* (Stanford, CA: Stanford University Press, 1999).
35 Michael R. Marrus and Robert O. Paxton, *Vichy France and the Jews* (New York: Basic Books, 1981), p. 3.
36 See Nicolas Weill, "La nasse administrative des fichiers sous Vichy," *Le Monde*, December 21, 1997.
37 See Marrus and Paxton, *Vichy France and the Jews*, pp. 241–5.
38 See Susan Zuccotti, *The Holocaust, the French, and the Jews* (New York: Basic Books, 1993), pp. 206–7.
39 For Baruch's testimony, see *Le procès de Maurice Papon*, 1: 415–36. See also Marc Olivier Baruch, *Servir l'État: l'administration en France de 1940 à 1944* (Paris: Fayard, 1997). For commentary on the book, see Annette Lèvy-Willard, "'Le vrai procès de la haute administration.' Pour Marc Olivier Baruch, Papon est typique de ces jeunes ambitieux qui font carrière sous Vichy," *Libération*, September 21,

1996, and Nicolas Weill, "Portrait d'une administration sur fond d'Occupation," *Le Monde*, November 5, 1997.
40 *Le procès de Maurice Papon*, 1: 420.
41 Ibid., 1: 314, 424, 390.
42 Ibid., 1: 405.
43 See Bertrand Poirot-Delpech, *Papon: un crime de bureau* (Paris: Stock, 1998), p. 104. See also Gérard Boulanger, *Maurice Papon: un technocrate français dans la collaboration* (Paris: Seuil, 1994).
44 See *Le procès de Maurice Papon*, 1: 862–72.
45 See Poirot-Delpech, *Papon: un crime de bureau*, pp. 120–2.
46 *Le procès de Maurice Papon*, 2: 428.
47 Ibid., 2: 431–2.
48 Ibid., 2: 199. In June 1943, when Alois Brunner took over as Commandant and reorganized the camp, detainee cadres drew up the lists of those to be deported.
49 *Le procès de Maurice Papon*, 1:493.
50 Ibid., 1: 498–9.
51 Ibid., 1: 500.
52 Michel Zaoui, *Mémoires de justice: Barbie, Touvier, Papon* (Paris: Seuil, 2009), p. 100.
53 See Sadat, "The Legal Legacy of Maurice Papon," p. 144.
54 See Adam Gopnik, "Papon's Paper Trial," *New Yorker*, April 27, 1998, p. 95.
55 Michel Zaoui, "Crimes contre l'humanité, conférence de Maître Michel Zaoui," http://www.cercleshoah.org/spip.php?article38.
56 Jean-Marie Colombani, "Savoir désobéir," *Le Monde*, April 4, 1998.
57 Gopnik, "Papon's Paper Trial," p. 95.
58 "Vél d'Hiv: M. Hollande réaffirme le rôle de la France," *Le Monde*, July 23, 2012.
59 Ibid.
60 Ibid. See also François Hollande, "The 'Crime Committed in France, by France,'" *New York Review of Books Daily*, August 18, 2012.

Chapter 2

1 Robert H. Jackson, *The Nürnberg Case* (New York: Knopf, 1947), pp. 97, 119. For a first-hand account of the proceedings, see Telford Taylor, *The Anatomy of the Nuremberg Trials: A Personal Memoir* (New York: Knopf, 1992).
2 See Bradley F. Smith, *Reaching Judgment at Nuremberg* (New York: Basic Books, 1977), pp. 163–5.
3 Jackson, *The Nürnberg Case*, p. 118.
4 See Hans W. Gatzke, *Stresemann and the Rearmament of Germany* (Baltimore, MD: Johns Hopkins University Press, 1954), ch. 2.

5. See Edward B. Westermann, "Hitler's Uniformed Police on the Eastern Front: The Reich's Secret Soldiers, 1941–1942," *War in History* 3 (1996): 309–29, and Christopher R. Browning, *Ordinary Men: Reserve Police Battalion 101 and the Final Solution in Poland*, rev. ed. (New York: Harper Perennial, 2017), ch. 2.
6. Browning, *Ordinary Men*, p. 11.
7. Ibid., pp. 11–12. Contrast Daniel Jonah Goldhagen's account in *Hitler's Willing Executioners: Ordinary Germans and the Holocaust* (New York: Knopf, 1996), pp. 181–91.
8. Browning, *Ordinary Men*, p. 39.
9. Ibid., p. 44.
10. Goldhagen, *Hitler's Willing Executioners*, pp. 207–8.
11. Browning, *Ordinary Men*, p. 48.
12. Ibid., p. 8.
13. Ibid., p. 57.
14. See ibid., p. 82.
15. Goldhagen, *Hitler's Willing Executioners*, pp. 228–9.
16. Ibid., p. 231.
17. Browning, *Ordinary Men*, p. 142.
18. Christopher R. Browning, "German Memory, Judicial Interrogation, and Historical Reconstruction: Writing Perpetrator History from Postwar Testimony," in Saul Friedländer, ed., *Probing the Limits of Representation: Nazism and the "Final Solution"* (Cambridge, MA: Harvard University Press, 1992), p. 30.
19. Christopher R. Browning, "Daniel Goldhagen's Willing Executioners," Selections from the Symposium, Holocaust Memorial Museum, Washington, D. C., April 8, 1996.
20. Browning, "German Memory, Judicial Interrogation, and Historical Reconstruction," p. 29.
21. Daniel Jonah Goldhagen, "The Evil of Banality," *New Republic* 207 (July 13–20, 1992): 49–52.
22. Browning, *Ordinary Men*, pp. 184–5.
23. Goldhagen. "The Evil of Banality."
24. Eleonore Sterling, *Judenhass: Die Anfänge des politischen Antisemitismus in Deutschland (1815–1850)* (Frankfurt: Europäische Verlagsanstalt, 1969), p. 121, quoted in Goldhagen, *Hitler's Willing Executioners*, p. 69.
25. Goldhagen, *Hitler's Willing Executioners*, pp. 69, 75.
26. Ibid., pp. 133, 87.
27. See ibid., p. 147n48.
28. Ibid., p. 158.
29. Browning, *Ordinary Men*, p. xx.
30. Goldhagen, "The Evil of Banality."
31. Volker Ullrich, "Die Deutschen—Hitlers willige Mordgesellen," *Die Zeit*, April 12, 1996.

32 A selection of the press coverage, in Germany and abroad, is collected in Juluis H. Schoeps, ed., *Ein Volk von Mördern? Die Dokumentation zur Goldhagen Kontroverse um die Rolle der Deutschen im Holocaust* (Hamburg: Hoffmann and Campe, 1997). See also Josef Joffe, "Goldhagen in Germany," *New York Review of Books*, November 28, 1996; Amos Elon, "The Antagonist as Liberator," *New York Times Magazine*, January 26, 1997; Mitchell G. Ash, "American and German Perspectives on the Goldhagen Debate: History, Identity, and the Media," *Holocaust and Genocide Studies* 11 (1997): 396–411; Bernard Rieger, "'Daniel in the Lion's Den?' The German Debate about Goldhagen's *Hitler's Willing Executioners*," *History Workshop Journal* 43 (1997): 226–33. A selection of readers' letters is collated in Daniel Jonah Goldhagen, ed., *Briefe an Goldhagen* (Berlin: Siedler, 1997).

33 Norbert Frei, "Ein Volk von 'Endlösern'?" in Schoeps, ed., *Ein Volk von Mördern?* pp. 89–92.

34 Eberhard Jäckel, "Einfach ein schlechtes Buch," in Schoeps, ed., *Ein Volk von Mördern?* pp. 187–92.

35 Hans Mommsen, "Die Antisemitismus war eine notwendige, aber keineswegs hinreichende Bedingung für Holocaust," *Die Zeit*, August 30, 1996.

36 Hans-Ulrich Wehler, "Wie ein Stachel im Fleisch," in Schoeps, ed., *Ein Volk von Mördern?* pp. 193–209.

37 Volker Ullrich, "Daniel J. Goldhagen in Deutschland: Die Buchtournee wurde Triumphzug," *Die Zeit*, September 13, 1996.

38 Alon, "The Antagonist as Liberator."

39 Ullrich, "Goldhagen in Deutschland."

40 Alon, "The Antagonist as Liberator."

41 Ibid.

42 Ullrich, "Goldhagen in Deutschland."

43 Joffe, "Goldhagen in Germany."

44 Ibid.

45 See Jürgen Habermas, "Über den öffentlichen Gebrauch der Historie: Warum ein 'Demokratiepreis' für Daniel J. Goldhagen? Eine Laudatio," *Die Zeit*, March 14, 1997.

46 Goldhagen, *Hitler's Willing Executioners*, p. 166n13.

47 Omer Bartov, *Germany's War and the Holocaust: Disputed Histories* (Ithaca, NY: Cornell University Press, 2003), p. 158.

48 Hannes Heer, "The Difficulty of Ending a War: Reactions to the Exhibition 'War of Extermination: Crimes of the Wehrmacht 1941–1944'," trans. Jane Caplan, *History Workshop Journal* 46 (1998): 189.

49 Omer Bartov, "German Soldiers and the Holocaust: Historiography, Research and Implications," *History and Memory* 9 (1997): 163. See also David Clay Lodge, *Germans to the Front: West German Rearmament in the Adenauer Era* (Chapel Hill: University of North Carolina Press, 1996), and Norbert Frei, *Adenauer's Germany*

and the Nazi Past: The Politics of Amnesty and Integration, trans. Joel Golb (New York: Columbia University Press, 2002).

50 Heer, "The Difficulty of Ending a War," p. 188.
51 Ibid. p. 188. See also *Vernichtungskrieg: Verbrechen der Wehrmacht 1941 bis 1944: Ausstellungskatalog* (Hamburg: Hamburger Edition, 1996). The exhibition was accompanied by an important collection of essays, edited by the organizers and written by leading scholars in the field: Hannes Heer and Klaus Naumann, eds., *Vernichtungskrieg: Verbrechen der Wehrmacht 1941–1944* (Hamburg: Hamburger Edition, 1995). For an English-language edition, see Hannes Heer and Klaus Naumann, eds., *War of Extermination: The German Military in World War II*, trans. Roy Shelton (New York: Berghahn Books, 2000).
52 See *Der Spiegel*, no. 11 (1997).
53 Karl-Heinz Janssen, "Als Soldaten Mörder Werden," *Die Zeit*, March 17, 1995. See also *Gehorsam bis zum Mord? Der verschwiegene Krieg der deutschen Wehrmacht—Fakten, Analysen, Debatte, Die Zeit, Zeitmagazin*, 1995.
54 Eve Rosenhaft, "Facing Up to the Past—Again?" *Debatte: Journal of Contemporary Central and Eastern Europe* 5 (1997): 107–8.
55 "Deutscher Bundestag, Stenographischer Bericht vom 13 März 1997," in Hans-Günther Thiele, ed., *Die Wehrmachtausstellung: Dokumentation eine Kontroverse* (Bremen: Edition Temmen, 1997), p. 195.
56 Ian Traynor, "Neo-Nazis Show Muscle," *Guardian*, March 3, 1997.
57 Heer, "The Difficulty of Ending a War," p. 196.
58 See Bill Niven, *Facing the Nazi Past: United Germany and the Legacy of the Third Reich* (London: Routledge, 2002), p. 162.
59 "Deutscher Bundestag, Stenographischer Bericht," pp. 181–2.
60 Ibid., pp. 191–2.
61 "Antrag der Fraktionen der CDU/CSU und FDP," in Thiele, ed., *Die Wehrsmachtausstellung*, p. 222.
62 See Samson Madievski, "The War of Extermination: The Crimes of the Wehrmacht in 1941 to 1944," trans. Olga Solonari, *Rethinking History* 7 (2003): 246. See also Volker Ullrich, "Von Bildern und Legenden," *Die Zeit*, October 28, 1999.
63 For the catalogue of the show that did not open, see Hamburg Institute for Social Research, ed., *The German Army and Genocide: Crimes against War Prisoners, Jews, and Other Civilians, 1939–1944* (New York: New Press, 1999).
64 Omer Bartov, "The Wehrmacht Exhibition Controversy: The Politics of Evidence," in Omer Bartov, Atina Grossman, and Mary Nolan, eds., *Crimes of War: Guilt and Denial in the Twentieth Century* (New York: New Press, 2002), p. 42.
65 Omer Bartov, et al., *Bericht, der Komission zur Überprüfung der Ausstellung "Vernichtungskrieg: Verbrechen der Wehrmacht 1941 bis 1944"* (November 2000), pp. 79, 85, quoted in Bartov, "The Wehrmacht Exhibition Controversy," p. 42. See

also Volker Ullrich, "Sie waren Mörder: Die Wehrmachtausstellung ist rehabilitiert," *Die Zeit*, November 16, 2000.
66. Hamburger Institut für Sozialforschung, ed., *Verbrechen der Wehrmacht: Dimensionen des Vernichtungskrieges 1941–1944: Ausstellungskatalog* (Hamburg: Hamburger Edition, 2001), p. 9.
67. See Hannes Heer, "The Head of Medusa," in Hannes Heer, Walter Manochek, Alexander Pollak, and Ruth Wodak, eds., *The Discursive Construction of History: Remembering the Wehrmacht's War of Annihilation*, trans. Steven Fligelstone (New York: Palgrave Macmillan, 2008), p. 241.
68. *Verbrechen der Wehrmacht: Ausstellungskatalog*, pp. 89–90. See also Omer Bartov, *Hitler's Army: Soldiers, Nazis, and War in the Third Reich* (New York: Oxford University Press, 1991), pp. 129–31.
69. Klaus Wiegrefe, "Abrechnung mit Hitlers' Generälen," *Der Spiegel*, no. 48 (2001), quoted in Heer, "The Head of Medusa," p. 240.
70. "Die Wehrmacht war keine Mörderbande," *Frankfurter Allgemeine Zeitung*, November 27, 2001, quoted in Heer, "The Head of Medusa," p. 240.
71. Madievski, "The War of Extermination," p. 250 (emphasis in the original).
72. Heidemarie Uhl, "Interpreting the 'War of Annihilation': Responses to the Exhibition 'Crimes of the Wehrmacht: Dimensions of a War of Annihilation, 1941 to 1944' When Staged in Vienna in 2002," in Heer et al., ed., *The Discursive Construction of History*, p. 258.
73. Michael Jeismann, "Das Ende der Wiedergänger," *Frankfurter Allgemeine Zeitung*, November 29, 2001, quoted in Heer, "The Head of Medusa," p. 247.
74. "Die Verweigerung von Argumentation," *Der Standard*, April 15, 2002, quoted in Heer, "The Head of Medusa," p. 247. See also Volker Ullrich, "Fragwürdiger Augenzeuge," *Die Zeit*, November 29, 2001, and Volker Ullrich and Norbert Frei, "Es ist nie zu Ende," *Die Zeit*, January 22, 2004.
75. David Denby, "Ordinary People," *The New Yorker*, February 3, 2014.
76. Ulrich Herbert, "'Unsere Mütter, unsere Väter': Die Nazis sind immer die anderen," *Die Tageszeitung*, March 21, 2013. See also Nicolas Büchse, Stefan Schmitz, and Matthias Weber, "Das gespaltene Urteil der Historiker," *Stern*, March 23, 2013.

Chapter 3

1. See Brian Ladd, *Ghosts of Berlin: Confronting German History in the Urban Landscape* (Chicago: University of Chicago Press, 1997), pp. 218–24.
2. Articles and speeches prompted by the Bitburg controversy are collected in Geoffrey H. Hartmann, ed., *Bitburg in Moral and Political Perspective* (Bloomington: University of Indiana Press, 1986).

3   See Bill Niven, *Facing the Nazi Past: United Germany and the Legacy of the Third Reich* (London: Routledge, 2002), pp. 197–200.
4   Norbert Lammert, foreword to *Holocaust Information Centre at the Memorial to the Murdered Jews of Europe* (Berlin: Foundation Memorial to the Murdered Jews of Europe, 2016), p. 7.
5   See Jörg Friedrich, *The Fire: The Bombing of Germany*, trans. Allison Brown (New York: Columbia University Press, 2006), and W. G. Sebald, *On the Natural History of Destruction*, trans. Anthea Bell (New York: Modern Library Paperback, 2004). The latter was originally published in German in a slightly different form as *Luftkrieg und Literatur*.
6   Martin Walser, "Experiences while Composing a Sunday Speech: The Peace Prize Speech" (1998), in Thomas A. Kovach and Martin Walser, *The Burden of the Past: Martin Walser on Modern German Identity and Texts, Contexts, and Commentary*, trans. Thomas A. Kovach (Rochester, NY: Camden House, 2008), pp. 89–91.
7   Niven, *Facing the Nazi Past*, p. 182. On the ensuing dispute between Walser, Bubis, and a host of commentators and letter writers, see Frank Schirrmacher, ed., *Die Walser-Bubis Debatte: Eine Dokumentation* (Frankfurt: Suhrkamp, 1999). For useful commentary, see Amir Eshel, "Vom eigenen Gewissen: Die Walser-Bubis Debatte und der Ort des Nationalsozialismus im Selbstbild der Bundesrepublik," *Deutsche Vierteljahrsschrift für Literaturwissenschaft und Geistesgeschichte* 74/2 (2000): 333–60.
8   Walser, "Sunday Speech," p. 91. After the Memorial was built, Walser said "on Vatican radio that he had made a terrible mistake in opposing it." Peter Eisenman, *The Leo Baeck Memorial Lecture, 49: Memorial to the Murdered Jews of Europe* (New York and Berlin: Leo Baeck Institute, 2005), p. 5.
9   Lea Rosh, "Ein Denkmal in Lande der Täter," in *Ein Denkmal für die ermordeten Juden Europas: Dokumentation 1988–1995* (Berlin: Bürgerinitiative Perspective Berlin e.V., 1995), p. 3, quoted in Caroline Wiedmer, *The Claims of Memory: Representations of the Holocaust in Contemporary Germany and France* (Ithaca, NY: Cornell University Press, 1999), p. 142. For a 1,200-page compendium of articles on the debate about the memorial, see Ute Heimrod, Günter Schlusche, and Horst Seferens, *Der Denkmalstreit—das Denkmal? Die Debatte um das "Denkmal für die ermordeten Juden Europas"—Eine Dokumentation* (Berlin: Philo, 1999).
10 See Ladd, *Ghosts of Berlin*, p. 170.
11 See Michael Z. Wise, *Capital Dilemma: Germany's Search for a New Architecture of Democracy* (New York: Princeton Architectural Press, 1998), p. 149.
12 James E. Young, *At Memory's Edge: After-Images of the Holocaust in Contemporary Art and Architecture* (New Haven, CT: Yale University Press, 2000), p. 189.
13 Ibid., p. 189.
14 Ibid., p. 191.

15 James E. Young. "Gegen das Denkmal für Erinnerung," in Amnon Barzel, et al., *Der Wettbewerb für das "Denkmal für die ermordeten Juden Europas": eine Streitschrift* (Berlin: Verlag der Kunst/Neue Gesellschaft für Bildende Kunst, 1995), pp. 174–8, quoted in Young, *At Memory's Edge*, p. 191.
16 See James E. Young, *The Texture of Memory: Holocaust Memorials and Meaning* (New Haven, CT: Yale University Press, 1993).
17 Young, *At Memory's Edge*, pp. 192, 193–4, 195.
18 Ibid., p. 195.
19 James E. Young, quoted in Michael Z. Wise, "Totem and Taboo: The New Berlin Struggle to Build a Holocaust Memorial," *Lingua Franca: The Review of Academic Life* 8/9 (December/January 1999): 39.
20 Young, *At Memory's Edge*, pp. 200, 203. See also Gavriel D. Rosenfeld, "Deconstructivism and the Holocaust: Peter Eisenman's Memorial to the Murdered Jews of Europe," in Claudio Fogu, Wulf Kansteiner, and Todd Presner, eds., *Probing the Ethics of Holocaust Culture* (Cambridge, MA: Harvard University Press, 2016), pp. 283–303, and Peter Eisenman, "Berlin Memorial Redux," in ibid., pp. 302–8.
21 James E. Young, "Peter Eisenman's Design for the Berlin Memorial for the Murdered Jews of Europe: A Juror's Report in Three Parts," in Robin Ostow, ed., *(Re)Visualizing National History: Museums and National Identities in the New Millennium* (Toronto: University of Toronto Press, 2008), p. 202n.
22 Ibid., pp. 203–4.
23 Young, *At Memory's Edge*, p. 217.
24 Sharon Chin, Fabian Franke, and Sheri Halpern, "A Self Serving Admission of Guilt: An Examination of the Intentions and Effects of Germany's Memorial to the Murdered Jews of Europe," www.humanityinaction.org/knowledgebase/225-a-self-serving-admission-of-guilt-an-examination-of-the-intentions-and-effects-of-germany-s-memorial-to-the-murdered-jews-of-europe, p. 4. See also Richard Brody, "The Inadequacy of Berlin's 'Memorial to the Murdered Jews of Europe,'" www.newyorker.com/culture/richard-brody/the-inadequacy-of-berlins-memorial-to-the-murdered-jews-of-europe; Caroline Gay, "The Politics of Remembrance: The Holocaust Monument in Berlin," *International Journal of Cultural Policy* 9/2 (2003): 153–66; Peter Carrier, *Holocaust Monuments and National Memory Culture in France and Germany since 1989: The Origins and Political Function of the Vél' d'Hiv' in Paris and the Holocaust Monument in Berlin* (New York: Berghahn Books, 2005); Irit Dekel, "Ways of Looking: Observation and Transformation at the Holocaust Memorial, Berlin," *Memory Studies* 2/1 (2009): 71–86.
25 See *Holocaust Information Centre*.
26 See Brigitte Sion, "Affective Memory, Ineffective Functionality: Experiencing Berlin's Memorial to the Murdered Jews of Europe," in Bill Niven and Chloe Paver,

eds., *Memorialization in Germany since 1945* (New York: Palgrave Macmillan, 2010), pp. 243–52.

27 Eisenman, *Leo Baeck Memorial Lecture*, p. 3.
28 Walser, "Sunday Speech," p. 91.
29 On Walser and Habermas and their generation, see A. Dirk Moses, *German Intellectuals and the Nazi Past* (Cambridge: Cambridge University Press, 2007).
30 Jürgen Habermas, "Der Zeigefinger: Die Deutschen und ihr Denkmal," *Die Zeit*, March 31, 1999.
31 Jürgen Habermas to Peter Eisenman, December 16, 1998, in Heimrod, et. al., *Der Denkmalstreit—das Denkmal?* p. 1185.
32 Sebald, *On the Natural History of Destruction*, pp. 3–4. The figures on casualties are open to question. Friedrich says that they are uncertain and vary between 420,000 and 570,000: *The Fire*, p. 50.
33 Richard Overy, *The Bombing War: Europe 1939–1945* (London: Penguin, 2014), p. 254.
34 National Archives, AIR 9/132, RE8 Report, "Consideration of the Types of Bombs for Specific Objectives Based on the Experience of German Bombing in this Country," September 26, 1940, pp. 2–3, quoted in Overy, *The Bombing War*, p. 256.
35 Charles Webster and Noble Frankland, *The Strategic Air Offensive against Germany*, 4 vols. (London: Her Majesty's Stationery Office, 1961), 4: 143–8, quoted in Overy, *The Bombing War*, p. 288.
36 Overy, *The Bombing War*, p. 334.
37 See ibid., pp. 335, 327.
38 Ibid., p. 395. See also Frederick Taylor, *Dresden, Tuesday February 13, 1945* (New York: HarperCollins, 2004), and Paul Addison and Jeremy A. Craig, eds., *Firestorm: The Bombing of Dresden 1945* (London: Pimlico, 2006).
39 Overy, *The Bombing War*, p. 408.
40 Gilad Margalit, *Guilt, Suffering, and Memory: Germany Remembers Its Dead of World War II*, trans. Haim Watzman (Bloomington: Indiana University Press, 2010), p. 265.
41 See Peter Schneider, "Deutsche as Opfer? Über ein Taboo der Nachkriegsgeneration," in Lothar Kettenacker, ed., *Ein Volk von Opfern? Die neue Debatte um den Bombenkrieg 1940–1945* (Berlin: Rowohlt, 2003), and Robert G. Moeller, "Germans as Victims? Thoughts on a Post-Cold War History of World War II: Legacies," *History and Memory* 17/1–2 (Spring–Winter 2005): 145–94. See also Bill Niven, ed., *Germans as Victims: Remembering the Past in Contemporary Germany* (New York: Palgrave Macmillan, 2006).
42 Sebald, *On the Natural History of Destruction*, pp. 145, 146.
43 Ibid., pp. 71, 70.
44 Ibid., p. 10.

45 Alfred Döblin, in Hans Magnus Enzenberger, *Europa in Trümmern* (Frankfurt: Eichborn, 1990), p. 188, quoted in Sebald, *The Natural History of Destruction*, p. 5.
46 Stig Dagerman, in Enzenberger, *Europa in Trümmern*, pp. 203 ff., quoted in Sebald, *The Natural History of Destruction*, p. 30 (emphasis in the original).
47 Sebald, *On the Natural History of Destruction*, p. 10.
48 Ibid., pp. 85, 93.
49 See Hans Erich Nossack, *The End: Hamburg 1943*, trans. Joel Agee (Chicago: University of Chicago Press, 2004).
50 Ibid., p. 70. See Jörg Friedrich, *Das Gesetz des Krieges: das deutsche Heer in Russland, 1941 bis 1945: der Prozess gegen das Oberkommando der Wehrmacht* (Munich: Piper, 1993), pp. 714–42.
51 Margalit, *Guilt, Suffering, and Memory*, p. 255.
52 Ibid., p. 257. The quotation is from *Bild*, September 13, 2002.
53 For a collection of some of the most important contributions to the debate surrounding *Der Brand*, see Kettenacker, ed., *Ein Volk von Opfern?*
54 Jörg Friedrich, *Brandstätten: Der Anblick des Bombenkrieges* (Munich: Propyläen, 2003). For thoughtful criticism, see Dietmar Suess, review of *Brandstätten: Der Anblick des Bombenkrieges*, by Jörg Friedrich, H-German, H-Net Reviews, November 2004. URL: http://www.h-net.org/reviews/showrev.php?id=10004.
55 See, for example, Jörg Arnold, review of *Der Brand: Deutschland in Bombenkrieg 1940–1945*, by Jörg Friedrich, H-German, H-Net Reviews, November 2003. URL: http://www.h-net.org/reviews.showrev.php?id=8358, and Douglas Pfeifer, review of *Der Brand: Deutschland in Bombenkrieg 1940–1945*, by Jörg Friedrich, H-German, H-Net Reviews, November 2003. URL: http://www.h-net.org/reviews/showrev.php?id=8365. See also Eric Langenbacher, "The Return of Memory: New Discussions about German Suffering in World War II," *German Society and Politics* 21/3 (2003): 74–88, and Jack R. Fischel, "Crimes of My Enemy," *The Virginia Quarterly Review* 83/1 (2007): 289–94.
56 Friedrich, *The Fire*, p. 296.
57 Ibid., pp. 49, 98, 386, 389.
58 Ibid., pp. 359, 379, 380.
59 Quoted in Friedrich, *The Fire*, p. 378. Friedrich gives no reference for his quotation.
60 See ibid., p. 379. Sebald's account is somewhat different: "[I]n the Altmarkt in Dresden, ... 6,865 corpses were burned on pyres in February 1945 by an SS detachment which had gained its experience at Treblinka." *Natural History of Destruction*, p. 98.
61 Friedrich, *The Fire*, p. 252.
62 Ian Buruma, "The Destruction of Germany," *New York Review of Books*, October 21, 2004.
63 Friedrich, *The Fire*, pp. 269, 93, 314.
64 See ibid., p. 146.

65 Andreas Hillgruber, *Zweierlei Untergang: Die Zerschlagung des Deutschen Reiches and das Ende des europäischen Judentums* (Berlin: Siedler, 1986), pp. 24–5.
66 Charles S. Maier, *The Unmasterable Past: History, Holocaust, and German National Identity* (Cambridge, MA: Harvard University Press, 1988), p. 23.
67 Günter Grass, *Crabwalk*, trans. Krishna Winston (Orlando, FL: Harcourt, 2003). Four years after the publication of *Crabwalk*, Grass produced his memoir *Beim Häuten der Zweibel* (*Peeling the Onion*). In it, he revealed that at age seventeen he had been drafted into the Waffen-SS. The righteous polemicist who criticized Germans' denial of their Nazi past had suppressed the fact of his personal involvement. In his telling, he manages to preserve an unknowing bewilderment, complicit, yet ignorant. See Günter Grass, *Peeling the Onion*, trans. Michael Henry Heim (London: Harvill Secker, 2007).
68 Robert G. Moeller, "Sinking Ships, the Lost Heimat and Broken Taboos: Günter Grass and the Politics of Memory in Contemporary Germany," *Contemporary European History* 12/2 (2003): 149.
69 Grass, *Crabwalk*, p. 13.
70 Ibid., p. 197.
71 J. M. Coetzee, "Victims," *New York Review of Books*, June 12, 2003.
72 Grass, *Crabwalk*, pp. 195, 204.
73 Ibid., pp. 198, 201–2.
74 Ibid., pp. 199, 200.

Chapter 4

1 Eberhard Jäckel, "The Impoverished Practice of Insinuation: The Singular Aspect of National-Socialist Crimes Cannot Be Denied," in *Forever in the Shadow of Hitler?: Original Documents of the "Historikerstreit," the Controversy Concerning the Singularity of the Holocaust*, trans. James Knowlton and Truett Cates (Atlantic Highlands, NJ: Humanities Press, 1993), pp. 76–7.
2 Major studies include Charles S. Maier, *The Unmasterable Past: History, Holocaust, and German National Identity* (Cambridge, MA: Harvard University Press, 1988); Richard J. Evans, *In Hitler's Shadow: West German Historians and the Attempt to Escape the Nazi Past* (New York: Pantheon, 1989); Peter Baldwin, ed., *Reworking the Past: Hitler, the Holocaust, and the Historians' Debate* (Boston: Beacon Press, 1990).
3 See Evans, *In Hitler's Shadow*, p. 122. See also "Forum: The *Historikerstreit* Twenty Years On," *German History* 24/4 (2006): 587–607. Andreas Hillgruber's *Zweierlei Untergang: Die Zerschlagung des Deutschen Reiches und das Ende des europäishen Judentums* (Berlin: Siedler, 1986) was also a trigger for Habermas's opening salvo.

4   Timothy Snyder, *Bloodlands: Europe between Hitler and Stalin* (New York: Basic Books, 2010).
5   H. Stuart Hughes, *Sophisticated Rebels: The Political Culture of European Dissent, 1968–1987* (Cambridge, MA: Harvard University Press, 1988), p. 122.
6   Jürgen Habermas, "On the Public Use of History," in Jürgen Habermas, *The New Conservatism: Cultural Criticism and the Historians' Debate,* ed. and trans. Shierry Weber Nicholsen (Cambridge, MA: MIT Press, 1989), pp. 236–7.
7   Ibid., p. 238.
8   See Ernst Nolte, *Three Faces of Fascism: Action Française, Italian Fascism, National Socialism,* trans. Leila Vennewitz (New York: Holt, Rinehart and Winston, 1965), and Ernst Nolte, *Deutschland und der kalte Krieg* (Munich: Piper, 1974).
9   Charles S. Maier, "The *Historikerstreit* in Context," in Baldwin, ed., *Reworking the Past,* p. 41.
10 Ernst Nolte, "The Past That Will Not Pass: A Speech That Could Be Written but Not Delivered," in *Forever in the Shadow of Hitler?* pp. 21–2.
11 Joachim Fest, "Encumbered Remembrance: The Controversy about the Incomparability of National Socialist Mass Crimes," in *Forever in the Shadow of Hitler?* p. 65.
12 Nolte, "The Past That Will Not Pass," p. 22.
13 Ernst Nolte, "Between Historical Legend and Revisionism? The Third Reich in the Perspective of 1980," in *Forever in the Shadow of Hitler?* p. 14.
14 François Furet and Ernst Nolte, *Fascism and Communism,* trans. Katherine Golsan (Lincoln: University of Nebraska Press, 2001), p. 86 (emphasis in the original).
15 See Saul Friedländer, *Nazi Germany and the Jews,* 2 vols. (New York: HarperCollins, 1997–2007). See also Alon Confino, "Narrative Form and Historical Sensation: On Saul Friedländer's *The Years of Extermination*," *History and Theory* 48/3 (2009): 199–219.
16 Saul Friedländer, *Where Memory Leads: My Life* (New York: Other Press, 2016), pp. 215–9.
17 Friedländer, *Nazi Germany and the Jews,* 1: 2.
18 Saul Friedländer, *Memory, History, and the Extermination of the Jews of Europe* (Bloomington: Indiana University Press, 1993), p. 132.
19 In keeping a diary throughout the Third Reich—to bear witness, "precise witness"—Klemperer exposed himself to grave danger. At the same time, it kept him more or less on an even keel. When, in 1995, a quarter-century after his death, an edited version of his diary went on sale, it was a sensation. In the year after its publication, it sold 125,000 hardcover copies and remained on German bestseller lists for over forty weeks. Victor Klemperer, *I Will Bear Witness: A Diary of the Nazi Years 1933–1945,* trans. Martin Chalmers, 2 vols. (New York: Random House, 1998–9), 2: May 27, 1942, p. 61. See also Amos Elon, "The Jew Who Fought to

Stay German," *New York Times Magazine*, March 26, 1996, and John Schmid, "An East German Publishing Coup," *New York Times*, October 7, 1996.

20 Victor Klemperer, *The Language of the Third Reich: LTI—Lingua Tertii Imperii: A Philologist's Notebook*, trans. Martin Brady (London: Continuum, 2006), p. 161. Klemperer also recounted this incident in his diary: see *I Will Bear Witness*, 2: January 12, 1942, pp. 4–5.

21 Klemperer, *Language of the Third Reich*, p. 164.

22 See Ernst Nolte, *Der europäische Bürgerkrieg, 1917–1945: Nationalsozialismus und Bolschevismus* (Berlin: Propyläen Verlag, 1987).

23 Friedländer, *Where Memory Leads*, p. 222.

24 Snyder, *Bloodlands*, p. xviii.

25 Ibid., pp. vii–viii, x.

26 Ibid., p. xi.

27 Ibid., p. 196.

28 Anne Applebaum, *Red Famine: Stalin's War on Ukraine* (New York: Doubleday, 2017), p. 90.

29 Snyder, *Bloodlands*, p. 26.

30 See Applebaum, *Red Famine*, p. 141.

31 Snyder, *Bloodlands*, p. 32.

32 Applebaum, *Red Famine*, p. 159.

33 Ibid., pp. 165, 167.

34 Snyder, *Bloodlands*, p. 42.

35 See ibid., p. 53.

36 Applebaum, *Red Famine*, p. xxvi (emphasis in the original).

37 Ibid., p. xxvii.

38 Ibid., pp. 350, xxvii. See also Philippe Sands, *East West Street: On the Origins of "Genocide" and "Crimes Against Humanity"* (New York: Knopf, 2016).

39 Snyder, *Bloodlands*, p. 54.

40 Ibid., p. 89.

41 See Terry Martin, "The Origins of Soviet Ethnic Cleansing," *Journal of Modern History* 70/4 (1998): 813–61, and James Morris, "The Polish Terror: Spy Mania and Ethnic Cleansing in the Great Terror," *Europe-Asia Studies* 56/5 (2004): 751–66.

42 Snyder, *Bloodlands*, p. 93.

43 Jörg Baberowski and Anselm Doering-Manteuffel, "The Quest for Order and the Pursuit of Terror: National Socialist Germany and the Stalinist Soviet Union as Multiethnic Empires," in Michael Geyer and Sheila Fitzpatrick, eds., *Beyond Totalitarianism: Stalinism and Nazism Compared* (Cambridge: Cambridge University Press, 2009), p. 214.

44 Snyder, *Bloodlands*, p. 103.

45 Ibid., pp. 103–4.

46 Ibid., pp. 111, 118.

47 Ibid., p. 149.
48 Ibid., pp. 128–9. See also Jan T. Gross, *Revolution from Abroad: The Soviet Conquest of Poland's Western Ukraine and Western Belorussia*, expanded ed. (Princeton, NJ: Princeton University Press, 2002), pp. 187–223.
49 Snyder, *Bloodlands*, pp. 125, 140.
50 Ibid., p. 127.
51 Ibid., p. 133.
52 Friedländer, *Nazi Germany and the Jews*, 2: 27–8.
53 Snyder, *Bloodlands*, p. 187.
54 Ibid., p. 162 (emphasis in the original).
55 See Christopher R. Browning, *The Origins of the Final Solution: The Evolution of Nazi Jewish Policy, September 1939–March 1942* (Lincoln: University of Nebraska Press, 2004), pp. 237–8. For the argument that the Holocaust in White Russia occurred as part of the Hunger Plan, see Christian Gerlach, *Kalkulierte Morde: Die deutsche Wirtschafts- und Vernichtungspolitik in Weissrussland, 1941 bis 1944* (Hamburg: Hamburger Edition, 1999). See also Alex J. Kay, *Exploitation, Resettlement, Mass Murder: Political and Economic Planning for German Occupation Policy in the Soviet Union, 1940–1941* (New York: Berghahn Books, 2006).
56 Snyder, *Bloodlands*, pp. 172, 173.
57 Richard J. Evans, *The Third Reich at War 1939–1945* (London: Allen Lane, 2008), p. 173.
58 Snyder, *Bloodlands*, p. 213.
59 Ibid., pp. 143, 144, 145.
60 Ibid., p. 160.
61 Friedländer, *Nazi Germany and the Jews*, 2: 189.
62 See Christian Gerlach, "The Wannsee Conference, the Fate of German Jews, and Hitler's Decision in Principle to Exterminate All European Jews," *Journal of Modern History* 70/4 (1998): 759–812. See also Christian Gerlach, *The Extermination of the European Jews* (Cambridge: Cambridge University Press, 2016), p. 82.
63 See Browning, *The Origins of the Final Solution*, pp. 309–433.
64 Friedländer, *Nazi Germany and the Jews*, 2: 287.
65 Snyder, *Bloodlands*, p. 388.
66 Friedlander, *Nazi Germany and the Jews*, 2: xix (emphasis in the original).
67 Snyder, *Bloodlands*, pp. 187, 189.

Chapter 5

1 See Peter Kenez, "Pogroms in Hungary, 1946," in Murray Baumgarten, Peter Kenez, and Bruce Thompson, eds., *Varieties of Antisemitism: History, Ideology, Discourse* (Newark, NJ: University of Delaware Press, 2009), pp. 233–4.

2. Jan T. Gross, *Fear: Anti-Semitism in Poland after Auschwitz: An Essay in Historical Interpretation* (New York: Random House, 2006), p. 36.
3. See ibid., pp. 81–117.
4. Jan T. Gross, *Revolution from Abroad: The Soviet Conquest of Poland's Western Ukraine and Western Belorussia*, expanded ed. (Princeton, NJ: Princeton University Press, 2002), p. 269.
5. See Paul Lendvai, *Anti-Semitism Without Jews: Communist Eastern Europe* (Garden City, NY: Doubleday, 1971), p. 324.
6. Tony Judt, *Postwar: A History of Europe since 1945* (New York: Penguin, 2005), p. 435.
7. Ibid., p. 822.
8. Mária M. Kovács, "The 1920 *Numerus Clausus* and the Anti-Jewish Legislation after 1938 in Hungary," in Judit Molnár, ed., *The Holocaust in Hungary: A European Perspective* (Budapest: Balassi Kiadó, 2005), p. 133.
9. See Randolph L. Braham, "Hungary," in David S. Wyman, ed., *The World Reacts to the Holocaust* (Baltimore, MD: Johns Hopkins University Press, 1996), p. 205.
10. For events in Hungary, see Randolph L. Braham, *The Politics of Genocide: The Holocaust in Hungary*, 3rd ed., 2 vols. (New York: Columbia University Press, 2016), and Christian Gerlach and Götz Aly, *Das letzte Kapitel: Realpolitik, Ideologie und der Mord an den ungarischen Juden 1944–1945* (Stuttgart: Deutsche Verlags-Anstalt, 2001). See also András Kovács "Hungarian Intentionalism: New Directions in the Historiography of the Hungarian Holocaust," in Randolph L. Braham and András Kovács, eds., *The Holocaust in Hungary: Seventy Years Later* (New York: Central European University Press, 2016), pp. 3–24. On the forced labor service, see Randolph L. Braham, *The Hungarian Labor Service System, 1939–1945* (New York: Columbia University Press, 1977), and Robert Rozett, *Conscripted Slaves: Hungarian Forced Laborers on the Eastern Front during the Second World War* (Jerusalem: Yad Vashem, 2013).
11. Hans Safrian, *Eichmann's Men*, trans. Ute Stargardt (Cambridge: Cambridge University Press, 2010), p. 204.
12. See Randolph L. Braham, "Hungarian Jews," in Yisrael Gutman and Michael Berenbaum, eds., *Anatomy of the Auschwitz Death Camp* (Bloomington: University of Indiana Press, 1994), p. 465.
13. From the flyer, "Double Occupation." In each room in the House of Terror there is a flyer, printed in Hungarian and English, which provides a narrative for the exhibition in that particular room.
14. From the flyer, "Changing Clothes."
15. István Rév, *Retroactive Justice: Prehistory of Post-Communism* (Stanford, CA: Stanford University Press, 2005), p. 291.
16. András Schiff, "Hungarians Must Face Their Nazi Past, Not Venerate It," *Guardian*, December 11, 2013.

17. Gábor Gyáni, "The Memory of Trianon as a Political Instrument in Hungary Today," in Alexei Miller and Maria Lipman, eds., *The Convolutions of Historical Politics* (Budapest and New York: Central European University Press, 2012), p. 105.
18. See "The Entanglement of Powers," *Economist*, August 31, 2019, pp. 15–8.
19. Elisabeth Zerofsky. "Viktor Orbán's Far-Right Vision for Europe," *New Yorker*, January 14, 2019, p. 47. See also, *Hungary Turns Its Back on Europe: Dismantling Culture, Education, Science and the Media in Hungary 2010–2019*. URL: http://oktatoihalozat.hu/wp-content/uploads/2020/03/angol.pdf.
20. See Paul A. Hanebrink, *In Defense of Christian Hungary: Religion, Nationalism, and Antisemitism, 1890–1944* (Ithaca, NY: Cornell University Press, 2006).
21. Quoted in Paul Lendvai, *Orbán: Hungary's Strongman* (Oxford: Oxford University Press, 2017), p. 195.
22. Ibid., p. 208.
23. Zerosky, "Viktor Orbán's Far-Right Vision for Europe," p. 45.
24. George Soros and Gregor Peter Schmitz, "'The EU Is on the Verge of Collapse'—An Interview," *New York Review of Books*, February 11, 2016.
25. See "Change of State: Poland under PiS," *Economist*, April 21, 2018, pp. 43–5. See also Rafal Pankowski, *The Populist Radical Right in Poland: The Patriots* (London: Routledge, 2010).
26. Jan T. Gross, "Poles Cry for 'Pure Blood' Again," *New York Times*, November 17, 2017.
27. Marc Santora and Joanna Berendt, "Mixing Politics and Piety, a Priest Seeks to Shape Poland's Future," *New York Times*, September 22, 2019. See also Brian Porter-Szűcs, *Faith and Fatherland: Catholicism, Modernity, and Poland* (New York: Oxford University Press, 2011), and Brian Porter-Szűcs, "The Triumph of National Communism," in Jo Harper, ed., *Poland's Memory Wars: Essays on Illiberalism* (Budapest and New York: Central European University Press, 2018), pp. 65–79.
28. Jan T. Gross, *Neighbors: The Destruction of the Jewish Community in Jedwabne, Poland* (New York: Penguin, 2002), p. 117. See also, Jan T. Gross, "A Tangled Web: Confronting Stereotypes Concerning Relations between Poles, Jews, and Communists," in István Deák, Jan T. Gross, and Tony Judt, eds., *The Politics of Retribution in Europe: World War II and Its Aftermath* (Princeton, NJ: Princeton University Press, 2000), pp. 74–129, and Jan T. Gross, "Neighbors: Annals of War," *New Yorker*, March 12, 2001, pp. 64–77. The book has been the subject of several follow-up volumes, the most important of which is Antony Polonsky and Joanna B. Michlic, eds., *The Neighbors Respond: The Controversy over the Jedwabne Massacre in Poland* (Princeton, NJ: Princeton University Press, 2004). For additional, useful, commentary, see John Connelly, "Poles and Jews: The Revisions of Jan T. Gross," *Contemporary European History* 11/4 (2002): 641–58; William W. Hagen, "A 'Potent Devilish Mixture' of Motives: Explanatory Strategy and Assignment of Meaning in Jan Gross's *Neighbors*," *Slavic Review* 61 (2002): 466–75; Janine P. Holc, "Working

Through Jan Gross's *Neighbors*," *Slavic Review* 61 (2002): 453–9; Norman H. Naimark, "The Nazis and the 'East': Jedwabne's Circle of Hell," *Slavic Review* 61 (2002): 476–82; Alexander B. Rossino, "Polish 'Neighbors' and German Invaders: Anti-Jewish Violence in the Białystok District during the Opening Weeks of Operation Barbarossa," *Polin: Studies in Polish Jewry* 16 (2003): 431–52; Darius Stola, "Jedwabne: Revisiting the Evidence and Nature of the Crime," *Holocaust and Genocide Studies* 17/1 (2003): 139–52; Marci Shore, "Conversing with Ghosts: Jedwabne, Żydokomuna, and Totalitarianism," *Kritika: Explorations in Russian and Eurasian History* 6/2 (2005): 345–74; Maciej Janowski, "Jedwabne, July 10, 1941: Debating the History of a Single Day," in Miller and Lipman, eds., *The Convolutions of Historical Politics*, pp. 59–89.

29 Anna Bikont, *The Crime and the Silence: Confronting the Massacre of Jews in Wartime Jedwabne*, trans. Alissa Valles (New York: Farrar, Straus and Giroux, 2015), p. 5.
30 Ibid., pp. 515, 520–1.
31 See ibid., pp. 15–16, and Gross, *Neighbors*, p. xviii.
32 Bikont, *The Crime and the Silence*, p. 521.
33 Ibid., pp. 522–3.
34 Ibid. pp. 8–9.
35 Ibid., pp. 202, 224. See also Konstanty Gebert, *Living in the Land of Ashes* (Kraków: Austeria Publishing House, 2008), pp. 133–48.
36 Quoted in Gebert, *Living in the Land of Ashes*, p. 128.
37 Bikont, *The Crime and the Silence*, p. 141.
38 "The Official Address Delivered by the President of the Republic of Poland, Mr. Aleksander Kwaśniewski On July 10, 2001, in Jedwabne, Poland."
39 Ruth Franklin, "The Epilogue," *New Republic*, October 2, 2006, p. 40.
40 Bikont, *The Crime and the Silence*, p. 240.
41 Quoted in L. Hoberman, "The Past Can Hold a Horrible Power: 'Aftermath' a Thriller Directed by Wladyslaw Pasikowski," *New York Times*, October 25, 2013.
42 Ibid.
43 Denise Grollmus, "In the Polish Aftermath," *Tablet Magazine*, April 16, 2013.
44 Quoted in Gerald Tishler, "When Academic Freedom and Freedom of Speech Confront Holocaust Denial and Group Libel: Comparative Perspectives," *Boston College Third World Law Journal* 8 (1988): 71, 74.
45 Lawrence Douglas, *The Memory of Judgment: Making Law and History in the Trials of the Holocaust* (New Haven, CT: Yale University Press, 2001), p. 220.
46 Elisabeth Zerofsky, "Memory Politics: Does Poland's Government Want to Rewrite the Country's Past?" *New Yorker*, July 30, 2018, p. 18.
47 "History Wars: Poland's Historical-Memory Law Is Divisive and Hurtful. That's the Point," *Economist*, February 10, 2018, p. 50. See also Jelana Subotić, *Yellow Star, Red Star: Holocaust Remembrance after Communism* (Ithaca, NY: Cornell University Press, 2019), pp. 205–6.

Conclusion

1. Quoted in James Angelos, "The New German Anti-Semitism," *New York Times Magazine*, May 21, 2019.
2. Quoted in Henry Rousso, *The Vichy Syndrome: History and Memory in France since 1944*, trans. Arthur Goldhammer (Cambridge, MA: Harvard University Press, 1991), p. 197.
3. Adam Nossiter, "Marine Le Pen Denies French Guilt for Rounding Up Jews," *New York Times*, April 10, 2017.
4. Charles King, "Hitler Usually Wins: On the Return of Individual Authoritarianism," *Times Literary Supplement*, December 15, 2017, p. 27.
5. Richard Hofstadter, *The Paranoid Style in American Politics and Other Essays* (New York: Knopf, 1965), pp. 14, 29–30.
6. Thomas Chatterton Williams, "The French Origins of 'You Will Not Replace Us,'" *New Yorker*, December 4, 2017, pp. 24, 30.
7. See Lea David, *The Past Can't Heal Us: The Dangers of Mandatory Memory in the Name of Human Rights* (Cambridge: Cambridge University Press, 2020).

Select Bibliography

Addison, Paul, and Jeremy A. Craig, eds. *Firestorm:The Bombing of Dresden 1945*. London: Pimlico, 2006.

Applebaum, Anne. *Red Famine: Stalin's War on Ukraine*. New York: Doubleday, 2017.

Arendt, Hannah. *The Origins of Totalitarianism*. New York: Harcourt, Brace, 1951.

Arendt, Hannah. *Eichmann in Jerusalem: A Report on the Banality of Evil*. Rev. and enlarged ed. New York: Penguin, 2006.

Arnold, Jörg. Review of *Der Brand: Deutschland in Bombenkrieg 1940–1945*, by Jörg Friedrich. H-German, H-Net Reviews, November 2003. URL: http://www.h-net.org/reviews.showrev.php?id=8358.

Ash, Mitchell G. "American and German Perspectives on the Goldhagen Debate: History, Identity, and the Media." *Holocaust and Genocide Studies* 11 (1997); 396–411.

Baberowski, Jörg, and Anselm Doering-Manteuffel. "The Quest for Order and the Pursuit of Terror: National Socialist Germany and the Stalinist Soviet Union as Multiethnic Empires." In *Beyond Totalitarianism: Stalinism and Nazism Compared*. Edited by Michael Geyer and Sheila Fitzpatrick. Cambridge: Cambridge University Press, 2009.

Baldwin, Peter, ed. *Reworking the Past: Hitler, the Holocaust, and the Historians' Debate*. Boston: Beason Press, 1990.

Bartov, Omer. *Hitler's Army: Soldiers, Nazis, and War in the Third Reich*. New York: Oxford University Press, 1991.

Bartov, Omer. "German Soldiers and the Holocaust: Historiography, Research and Implications." *History and Memory* 9 (1997): 162–88.

Bartov, Omer. "The Wehrmacht Exhibition Controversy: The Politics of Evidence." In *Crimes of War: Guilt and Denial in the Twentieth Century*. Edited by Omer Bartov, Atina Grossman, and Mary Nolan. New York: New Press, 2002.

Bartov, Omer. *Germany's War and the Holocaust: Disputed Histories*. Ithaca, NY: Cornell University Press, 2003.

Bartov, Omer. "Eastern Europe as the Site of Genocide." *Journal of Modern History* 80/3 (2008): 557–93.

Baruch, Marc Olivier. *Servir l'État: l'administration en France de 1940 à 1944*. Paris: Fayard, 1997.

Berkhoff, Karel C. *Harvest of Despair: Life and Death in Ukraine under Nazi Rule*. Cambridge, MA: Harvard University Press, 2004.

Bikont, Anna. *The Crime and the Silence: Confronting the Massacre of Jews in Wartime Jedwabne*. Translated by Alissa Valles. New York: Farrar, Straus and Giroux, 2015.

Blobaum, Robert, ed. *Antisemitism and Its Opponents in Modern Poland*. Ithaca, NY: Cornell University Press, 2005.

Bloxham, Donald. *Genocide on Trial: War Crimes Trials and the Formation of Holocaust History and Memory*. Oxford: Oxford University Press, 2001.

Boulanger, Gérard. *Maurice Papon: un technocrate français dans la collaboration*. Paris: Seuil, 1994.

Braham, Randolph L. *The Hungarian Labor System, 1939–1945*. New York: Columbia University Press, 1977.

Braham, Randolph L. "Hungarian Jews." In *Anatomy of the Auschwitz Death Camp*. Edited by Yisrael Gutman and Michael Berenbaum. Bloomington: University of Indiana Press, 1994.

Braham, Randolph L. "Hungary." In *The World Reacts to the Holocaust*. Edited by David S. Wyman. Baltimore, MD: Johns Hopkins University Press, 1996.

Braham, Randolph L., ed. *The Treatment of the Holocaust in Hungary and Rumania during the Post-Communist Era*. New York: Columbia University Press, 2004.

Braham, Randolph L. *The Politics of Genocide: The Holocaust in Hungary*. 3rd ed., 2 vols. New York: Columbia University Press, 2016.

Brandon, Ray, and Wendy Lower, eds. *The Shoah in Ukraine: History, Testimony, Memorialization*. Bloomington: Indiana University Press, 2008.

Brody, Richard. "The Inadequacy of Berlin's 'Memorial to the Murdered Jews of Europe.'" www.newyorker.com/culture/richard-brody/the-inadequacy-of-berlins-memorial-to-the-murdered-jews-of-europe.

Browning, Christopher R. "German Memory, Judicial Interrogation, and Historical Reconstruction: Writing Perpetrator History from Postwar Testimony." In *Probing the Limits of Representation: Nazism and the "Final Solution."* Edited by Saul Friedländer. Cambridge, MA: Harvard University Press, 1992.

Browning, Christopher R. "Daniel Goldhagen's Willing Executioners." Selections from the Symposium. Holocaust Memorial Museum, Washington, D. C., April 8, 1996.

Browning, Christopher R. *Collected Memories: Holocaust History and Postwar Testimony*. Madison: University of Wisconsin Press, 2003.

Browning, Christopher R. *The Origins of the Final Solution: The Evolution of Nazi Jewish Policy, September 1939–March 1942*. Lincoln: University of Nebraska Press, 2004.

Browning, Christopher R. *Ordinary Men: Reserve Police Battalion 101 and the Final Solution in Poland*. Rev. ed. New York: Harper Perennial, 2017.

Bunzl, Matti. *Anti-semitism and Islamophobia: Hatreds Old and New In Europe*. Chicago: Prickly Paradigm Press, 2007.

Buruma, Ian. "The Destruction of Germany." *New York Review of Books*, October 21, 2004.

Camus, Jean-Yves, and Nicolas Lebourg. *Far-Right Politics in Europe*. Translated by Jane Marie Todd. Cambridge, MA: Harvard University Press, 2017.

Caron, Vicki. *Uneasy Asylum: France and the Jewish Refugee Crisis, 1933–1942*. Stanford, CA: Stanford University Press, 1999.

Carrier, Peter. *Holocaust Monuments and National Memory Culture in France and Germany since 1989: The Origins and Political Function of the Vél' d'Hiv' in Paris and the Holocaust Monument in Berlin.* New York: Berghahn Books, 2005.

Chin, Sharon, Fabian Franke, and Sheri Halpern, "A Self Serving Admission of Guilt: An Examination of the Intentions and Effects of Germany's Memorial to the Murdered Jews of Europe." www.humanityinaction.org/knowledgebase/225-a-self-serving-admission-of-guilt-an-examination-of-the-intentions-and-effects-of-germany-s-memorial-to-the-murdered-jews-of-europe.

Coetzee, J. M. "Victims." *New York Review of Books*, June 12, 2003.

Cohen, William B. "The Algerian War, the French State and Official Memory." *Historical Reflections/Réflexions Historiques* 28 (2002): 219–39.

Conan, Éric. *Le procès Papon: un journal d'audience.* Paris: Gallimard, 1998.

Conan, Éric, and Henry Rousso. *Vichy: An Ever-Present Past.* Translated by Nathan Bracher. Hanover, NH: University Press of New England, 1998.

Confino, Alon. "Narrative Form and Historical Sensation: On Saul Friedländer's *The Years of Extermination*." *History and Theory* 48/3 (2009): 199–219.

Connelly, John. "Poles and Jews: The Revisions of Jan T. Gross." *Contemporary European History* 11/4 (2002): 641–58.

Craig, Gordon. "The War of the German Historians." *New York Review of Books*, January 17, 1987.

Crew, David F. *Bodies and Ruins: Imagining the Bombing of Germany, 1945 to the Present.* Ann Arbor: University of Michigan Press, 2017.

David, Lea. *The Past Can't Heal Us: The Dangers of Mandatory Memory in the Name of Human Rights.* Cambridge: Cambridge University Press, 2020.

Deák, István. "Holocaust Views: The Goldhagen Controversy in Retrospect." *Central European History* 30 (1997): 295–307.

Dekel, Irit. "Ways of Looking: Observation and Transformation at the Holocaust Memorial, Berlin." *Memory Studies* 2/1 (2009): 71–86.

Denby, David. "Ordinary People." *The New Yorker*, February 3, 2014.

Der Spiegel (Hambrug)

Die Tageszeitung (Berlin)

Die Zeit (Hamburg)

Douglas, Lawrence. *The Memory of Judgment: Making Law and History in the Trials of the Holocaust.* New Haven, CT: Yale University Press, 2001.

Ehrenberg, Ilya, and Vasily Grossman. *The Complete Black Book of Russian Jewry.* Edited and translated by David Patterson. New Brunswick, NJ: Transaction Publishers, 2002.

Einaudi, Jean-Luc. *La bataille de Paris: 17 octobre 1961.* Paris: Seuil, 1991.

Eisenman, Peter. *The Leo Baeck Memorial Lecture, 49: Memorial to the Murdered Jews of Europe.* New York and Berlin: Leo Baeck Institute, 2005.

Eley, Geoff. "Nazism, Politics and the Image of the Past: Thoughts on the West German Historikerstreit 1986–1987." *Past and Present* 121 (1988): 171–208.

Eley, Geoff, ed. *The "Goldhagen Effect": History, Memory, Nazism–Facing the German Past*. Ann Arbor: University of Michigan Press, 2000.

Elon, Amos. "The Jew Who Fought to Stay German." *New York Times Magazine*, March 26, 1996.

Elon, Amos. "The Antagonist as Liberator." *New York Times Magazine*, January 26, 1997.

Eshel, Amir. "Vom eigenen Gewissen: Die Walser-Bubis Debatte und der Ort des Nationalsozialismus im Selbstbild der Bundesrepublik." *Deutsche Vierteljahrsschrift für Literaturwissenschaft und Geistesgeschichte* 74/2 (2000): 333–60.

Evans, Richard J. *In Hitler's Shadow: West German Historians and the Attempt to Escape the Nazi Past*. New York: Pantheon, 1989.

Evans, Richard J. *Lying About Hitler: History, Holocaust, and the David Irving Trial*. New York: Basic Books, 2001.

Evans, Richard J. "History, Memory and the Law: The Historian as Expert Witness." *History and Theory* 41 (2002): 326–45.

Evans, Richard J. *The Third Reich at War 1939–1945*. London: Allen Lane, 2008.

Fest, Joachim. *Not I: Memoirs of a German Childhood*. Translated by Martin Chalmers. New York: Other Press, 2014.

Finkelstein, Norman G. *The Holocaust Industry: Reflections on the Exploitation of Jewish Suffering*. London: Verso, 2000.

Finkielkraut, Alain. *Remembering in Vain: The Klaus Barbie Trial and Crimes against Humanity*. Translated by Roxanne Lapidus and Sima Godfrey. New York: Columbia University Press, 1992.

Fischel, Jack R. "Crimes of My Enemy." *The Virginia Quarterly Review* 83/1 (2007): 289–94.

Forever in the Shadow of Hitler? Original Documents of the "Historikerstreit," the Controversy Concerning the Singularity of the Holocaust. Translated by James Knowlton and Truett Cates. Atlantic Highlands, NJ: Humanities Press, 1993.

"Forum: The *Historikerstreit* Twenty Years On." *German History* 24/4 (2006): 587–607.

Frankfurter Allgemeiner Zeitung.

Franklin, Ruth. "The Epilogue." *New Republic*, October 2, 2006.

Franzen, Erik K. *Die Vertriebenen: Hitlers letzte Opfer*. Munich: Ullstein, 2002.

Frei, Norbert. "Ein Volk von 'Endlösern'?" In *Ein Volk von Mördern? Die Dokumentation zur Goldhagen Kontroverse um die Rolle der Deutschen im Holocaust*. Edited by Julius H. Schoeps. Hamburg: Hoffmann and Campe, 1997.

Frei, Norbert. "Farewell to the Era of Contemporaries: National Socialism and Its Historical Examination en route into History." *History and Memory* 9 (1997): 59–79.

Frei, Norbert. *Adenauer's Germany and the Nazi Past: The Politics of Amnesty and Integration*. Translated by Joel Golb. New York: Columbia University Press, 2002.

Frei, Norbert. *1945 und wir: Das Dritte Reich im Bewusstsein des Deutschen*. Munich: Verlag C. H. Beck, 2005.

Frei, Norbert, ed. *Martin Broszat, der "Staat Hitlers" und die Historisierung des Nationalsozialismus*. Göttingen: Wallstein, 2007.

Friedländer, Saul. *When Memory Comes*. Translated by Helen R. Lane. New York: Farrar, Straus and Giroux, 1979.
Friedländer, Saul. *Memory, History, and the Extermination of the Jews of Europe*. Bloomington: Indiana University Press, 1993.
Friedländer, Saul. *Nazi Germany and the Jews*. 2 vols. New York: HarperCollins, 1997–2007.
Friedländer, Saul. *Where Memory Leads: My Life*. New York: Other Press, 2016.
Friedrich, Jörg, *Das Gesetz des Krieges: das deutsche Heer in Russland, 1941 bis 1945: der Prozess gegen das Oberkommando der Wehrmacht*. Munich: Piper, 1993.
Friedrich, Jörg. *Brandstätten: Der Anblick des Bombenkrieges*. Munich: Propyläen, 2003.
Friedrich, Jörg. *The Fire: The Bombing of Germany*. Translated by Allison Brown. New York: Columbia University Press, 2006.
Fullbrook, Mary. *German National Identity after the Holocaust*. Cambridge: Polity Press, 1999.
Furet, François, and Ernst Nolte. *Fascism and Communism*. Translated by Katherine Golsan. Lincoln: University of Nebraska Press, 2001.
Gatzke, Hans W. *Stresemann and the Rearmament of Germany*. Baltimore, MD: Johns Hopkins University Press, 1954.
Gay, Caroline. "The Politics of Remembrance: The Holocaust Monument in Berlin." *International Journal of Cultural Policy* 9/2 (2003): 153–66.
Gebert, Konstanty. *Living in the Land of Ashes*. Kraków: Austeria Publishing House, 2008.
Gehorsam bis zum Mord? Der verschwiegene Krieg der deutschen Wehrmacht—Fakten, Analysen, Debatte. Die Zeit, Zeitmagazin, 1995.
Gerlach, Christian. "The Wannsee Conference, the Fate of German Jews, and Hitler's Decision in Principle to Exterminate All European Jews." *Journal of Modern History* 70/4 (1998): 759–812.
Gerlach, Christian. *Kalkulierte Morde: Die deutsche Wirtschafts- und Vernichtungspolitik in Weissrussland, 1941 bis 1944*. Hamburg: Hamburger Edition, 1999.
Gerlach, Christian. *The Extermination of the European Jews*. Cambridge: Cambridge University Press, 2016.
Gerlach, Christian, and Götz Aly. *Das letzte Kapitel: Realpolitik, Ideologie und der Mord an den ungarishen Juden 1944–1945*. Stuttgart: Deutsche Verlags-Anstalt, 2001.
Goldhagen, Daniel Jonah. "The Evil of Banality." *New Republic* 207 (July 13–20, 1992): 49–52.
Goldhagen, Daniel Jonah. *Hitler's Willing Executioners: Ordinary Germans and the Holocaust*. New York: Knopf, 1996.
Goldhagen, Daniel Jonah, ed. *Briefe an Goldhagen*. Berlin: Siedler, 1997.
Golsan, Richard J. *Vichy's Afterlife: History and Counterhistory in Postwar France*. Lincoln: University of Nebraska Press, 2000.
Goltermann, Svenja. *The War in Their Minds: German Soldiers and Their Violent Pasts in West Germany*. Translated by Philip Schmitz. Ann Arbor: University of Michigan Press, 2017.

Gopnik, Adam. "Papon's Paper Trial." *New Yorker*, April 27, 1998.
Grabowski, Jan. *Hunt for the Jews: Betrayal and Murder in German-Occupied Poland.* Bloomington: Indiana University Press, 2013.
Grass, Günter. *The Tin Drum.* Translated by Ralph Manheim. New York: Pantheon, 1961.
Grass, Günter. *Cat and Mouse.* Translated by Ralph Manheim. Orlando, FL: Harcourt, 1963.
Grass, Günter. *Dog Years.* Translated by Ralph Manheim. New York: Harcourt, Brace and World, 1965.
Grass, Günter. *Crabwalk.* Translated by Krishna Winston. Orlando, FL: Harcourt, 2003.
Grass, Günter. *Peeling the Onion.* Translated by Michael Henry Heim. London: Harvill Secker, 2007.
Grollmus, Denise. "In the Polish Aftermath." *Tablet Magazine*, April 16, 2013.
Gross, Jan T. "A Tangled Web: Confronting Stereotypes Concerning Relations between Poles, Jews, and Communists." In *The Politics of Retribution in Europe: World War II and Its Aftermath*. Edited by István Deák, Jan T. Gross, and Tony Judt. Princeton, NJ: Princeton University Press, 2000.
Gross, Jan T. "Neighbors: Annals of War." *New Yorker*, March 12, 2001.
Gross, Jan T. *Neighbors: The Destruction of the Jewish Community in Jedwabne, Poland.* New York: Penguin, 2002.
Gross, Jan T. *Revolution from Abroad: The Soviet Conquest of Poland's Western Ukraine and Western Belorussia.* Expanded ed. Princeton, NJ: Princeton University Press, 2002.
Gross, Jan T. *Fear: Anti-Semitism in Poland after Auschwitz: An Essay in Historical Interpretation.* New York: Random House, 2006.
Gross, Jan T. "Opportunistic Killings and Plunder of Jews by Their Neighbors—a Norm or an Exception in German Occupied Europe?" In *Years of Persecution, Years of Extermination: Saul Friedländer and the Future of Holocaust Studies.* Edited by Christian Wiese and Paul Betts. London: Continuum, 2010.
Gross, Jan Tomasz, and Irena Grudzińska Gross. *Golden Harvest: Events on the Periphery of the Holocaust.* New York: Oxford University Press, 2012.
Guardian (London)
Gyáni, Gábor. "The Memory of Trianon as a Political Instrument in Hungary Today." In *The Convolutions of Historical Politics.* Edited by Alexei Miller and Maria Lipman. Budapest and New York: Central European University Press, 2012.
Habermas, Jürgen. *The New Conservatism: Cultural Criticism and the Historians' Debate.* Edited and translated by Shierry Weber Nicholsen. Cambridge, MA: MIT Press, 1989.
Hagen, William W. "A 'Potent Devilish Mixture' of Motives: Explanatory Strategy and Assignment of Meaning in Jan Gross's *Neighbors*." *Slavic Review* 61 (2002): 466–75.
Hamburg Institute for Social Research, ed., *The German Army and Genocide: Crimes against War Prisoners, Jews, and Other Civilians, 1939–1944.* New York: New Press, 1999.

Hamburger Institut für Sozialforschung, ed., *Verbrechen der Wehrmacht: Dimensionen des Vernichtungskrieges 1941–1944: Ausstellungskatalog*. Hamburg: Hamburger Edition, 2001.

Hanebrink, Paul A. *In Defense of Christian Hungary: Religion, Nationalism, and Antisemitism, 1890–1944*. Ithaca, NY: Cornell University Press, 2006.

Hanebrink, Paul A. *A Specter Haunting Europe: The Myth of Judeo-Bolshevism*. Cambridge, MA: Harvard University Press, 2018.

Hartmann, Geoffrey H., ed. *Bitburg in Moral and Political Perspective*. Bloomington: University of Indiana Press, 1986.

Heer, Hannes. "The Difficulty of Ending a War: Reactions to the Exhibition 'War of Extermination: Crimes of the Wehrmacht 1941–1944.'" Translated by Jane Caplan. *History Workshop Journal* 46 (1998): 187–203.

Heer, Hannes. "The Head of Medusa." In *The Discursive Construction of History: Remembering the Wehrmacht's War of Annihilation*. Edited by Hannes Heer, Walter Manochek, Alexander Pollak, and Ruth Wodak. Translated by Steven Fligelstone. New York: Palgrave Macmillan, 2008.

Heer, Hannes, and Klaus Naumann, eds. *Vernichtungskrieg: Verbrechen der Wehrmacht 1941–1944*. Hamburg: Hamburger Edition, 1995.

Heer, Hannes, and Klaus Naumann, eds. *War of Extermination: The German Military in World War II*. Translated by Roy Shelton. New York: Berghahn Books, 2000.

Heimrod, Ute, Günter Schlusche, and Horst Seferens. *Der Denkmalstreit—das Denkmal? Die Debatte um das "Denkmal für die ermordeten Juden Europas"—Eine Dokumentation*. Berlin: Philo, 1999.

Herczl, Moshe Y. *Christianity and the Holocaust of Hungarian Jewry*. Translated by Joel Lerner. New York: New York University Press, 1993.

Herf, Jeffrey. *Divided Memory: The Nazi Past in the Two Germanys*. Cambridge, MA: Harvard University Press, 1997.

Hilberg, Raul. *Perpetrators Victims Bystanders: The Jewish Catastrophe 1933–1945*. New York: HarperCollins, 1992.

Hilberg, Raul. *The Destruction of the European Jews*. 3 vols. New Haven, CT: Yale University Press, 2003.

Hillgruber, Andreas. *Zweierlei Untergang: Die Zerschlagung des Deutschen Reiches und das Ende des europäischen Judentums*. Berlin: Siedler, 1986.

Hinsey, Ellen. *Mastering the Past: Contemporary Central and Eastern Europe and the Rise of Illiberalism*. Candor, NY: Telos Press, 2017.

Hirshfeld, Gerhard. *The Politics of Genocide: Jews and Soviet Prisoners of War in Nazi Germany*. London: Allen and Unwin, 1986.

Hofstadter, Richard. *The Paranoid Style in American Politics and Other Essays*. New York: Knopf, 1965.

Holc, Janine P. "Working Through Jan Gross's *Neighbors*." *Slavic Review* 61 (2002): 453–9.

Hollande, François. "The 'Crime Committed in France, by France.'" *New York Review of Books Daily*, August 18, 2012.

House, Jim, and Neil MacMaster. "'Une Journée Portée Disparue': The Paris Massacre of 1961 and Memory." In *Crisis and Renewal in France*. Edited by Kenneth Mouré and Martin S. Alexander. New York: Berghahn Books, 2008.

Hughes, H. Stuart. *Sophisticated Rebels: The Political Culture of European Dissent, 1968–1987*. Cambridge, MA: Harvard University Press, 1988.

Hughes, Judith M. *The Holocaust and the Revival of Psychological History*. New York: Cambridge University Press, 2015.

Hughes, Judith M. *Witnessing the Holocaust: Six Literary Testimonies*. London: Bloomsbury, 2018.

Hungary Turns Its Back on Europe: Dismantling Culture, Education, Science and the Media in Hungary 2010–2019. URL: http://oktatoihalozat.hu/wp-content/uploads/2020/03/angol.pdf.

Jäckel, Eberhard. "Einfach ein schlechtes Buch." In *Ein Volk von Mördern? Die Dokumentation zur Goldhagen Kontroverse um die Rolle der Deutschen im Holocaust*. Edited by Julius H. Schoeps. Hamburg: Hoffmann and Campe, 1997.

Jackson, Robert H. *The Nürnberg Case*. New York: Knopf, 1947.

Janowski, Maciej. "Jedwabne, July 10, 1941: Debating the History of a Single Day." In *The Convolutions of Historical Politics*. Edited by Alexei Miller and Maria Lipman. Budapest and New York: Central European University Press, 2012.

Jarausch, Konrad H., and Michael Geyer. *Shattered Past: Reconstructing German Histories*. Princeton, NJ: Princeton University Press, 2003.

Joffe, Josef. "Goldhagen in Germany." *New York Review of Books*, November 28, 1996.

Judt, Tony. *Postwar: A History of Europe since 1945*. New York: Penguin, 2005.

Kay, Alex J. *Exploitation, Resettlement, Mass Murder: Political and Economic Planning for German Occupation Policy in the Soviet Union, 1940–1941*. New York: Berghahn Books, 2006.

Kenez, Peter. "Pogroms in Hungary, 1946." In *Varieties of Antisemitism: History, Ideology Discourse*. Edited by Murray Baumgarten, Peter Kenez, and Bruce Thompson. Newark, NJ: University of Delaware Press, 2009.

Kershaw, Ian. *Hitler*. 2 vols. New York: Norton, 1999–2000.

Kershaw, Ian. *Hitler, the Germans, and the Final Solution*. New Haven, CT: Yale University Press, 2008.

Kettenacker, Lothar, ed. *Ein Volk von Opfern? Die neue Debatte um den Bombenkrieg 1940–1945*. Berlin: Rowohlt, 2003.

King, Charles. "Hitler Usually Wins: On the Return of Individual Authoritarianism." *Times Literary Supplement*, December 17, 2017.

Kirchick, James. *The End of Europe: Dictators, Demagogues, and the Coming Dark Age*. New Haven, CT: Yale University Press, 2017.

Klarsfeld, Beate, and Serge Klarsfeld. *Hunting the Truth: Memoirs of Beate and Serge Klarsfeld*. Translated by Sam Taylor. New York: Farrar, Straus and Giroux, 2018.

Klarsfeld, Serge. *The Children of Izieu: A Human Tragedy*. Translated by Kenneth Jacobson. New York: H. Abrams, 1985.

Klemperer, Victor. *I Will Bear Witness: A Diary of the Nazi Years 1933–1945*. Translated by Martin Chalmers. 2 vols. New York: Random House, 1998–9.

Klemperer, Victor. *The Language of the Third Reich: LTI—Lingua Tertii Imperii: A Philologist's Notebook*. Translated by Martin Brady. London: Continuum, 2006.

Knopp, Guido. *Die grosse Flucht: Das Schicksal der Vertriebenen*. Munich: Ullstein, 2002.

Kohut, Thomas August. *A German Generation: An Experiential History of the Twentieth Century*. New Haven, CT: Yale University Press, 2012.

Kovács, András. "Hungarian Intentionalism: New Directions in the Historiography of the Hungarian Holocaust." In *The Holocaust in Hungary: Seventy Years Later*. Edited by Randolph L. Braham. New York: Central European University Press, 2016.

Kovács, Maria M. "The 1920 *Numerus Clausus* and the Anti-Jewish Legislation after 1938 in Hungary." In *The Holocaust in Hungary: A European Perspective*. Edited by Judit Molnar. Budapest: Balassi Kiadó, 2005.

Laczó, Ferenc. *Hungarian Jews in the Age of Genocide: An Intellectual History, 1929–1948*. Leiden: Brill, 2016.

Ladd, Brian. *Ghosts of Berlin: Confronting German History in the Urban Landscape*. Chicago: University of Chicago Press, 1997.

Lammert, Norbert. Foreword to *Holocaust Information Centre at the Memorial to the Murdered Jews of Europe*. Berlin: Foundation Memorial to the Murdered Jews of Europe, 2016.

Langenbacher, Eric. "The Return of Memory: New Discussions about German Suffering in World War II." *German Society and Politics* 21/3 (2003): 74–88.

Le Monde (Paris)

Le procès de Maurice Papon: compte rendu sténographique. 2 vols. Paris: Albin Michel, 1998.

Lendvai, Paul. *Anti-Semitism Without Jews: Communist Eastern Europe*. Garden City, NY: Doubleday, 1971.

Lendvai, Paul. *Orbán: Hungary's Strongman*. Oxford: Oxford University Press, 2017.

Lipstadt, Deborah E. *Denying the Holocaust: The Growing Assault on Truth and Memory*. New York: Free Press, 1993.

Lipstadt, Deborah E. *History on Trial: My Day in Court with a Holocaust Denier*. New York: Harper Perennial, 2006.

Lodge, David Clay. *Germans to the Front: West German Rearmament in the Adenauer Era*. Chapel Hill: University of North Carolina Press, 1996.

Madievski, Samson. "The War of Extermination: The Crimes of the Wehrmacht in 1941 to 1944." Translated by Olga Solonari. *Rethinking History* 7 (2003): 243–54.

Maier, Charles S. *The Unmasterable Past: History, Holocaust, and German National Identity*. Cambridge, MA: Harvard University Press, 1988.

Margalit, Gilad. *Guilt, Suffering, and Memory: Germany Remembers Its Dead of World War II*. Translated by Haim Watzman. Bloomington: Indiana University Press, 2010.

Marrus, Michael R., and Robert O. Paxton. *Vichy France and the Jews*. New York: Basic Books, 1981.

Martin, Terry. "The Origins of Soviet Ethnic Cleansing." *Journal of Modern History* 70/4 (1998): 813–61.

Mayer, Arno J. *Why Did the Heavens Not Darken? The "Final Solution" in History*. New York: Pantheon, 1988.

Mazower, Mark. *Hitler's Empire: How the Nazis Ruled Europe*. New York: Penguin, 2008.

Moeller, Robert G. "Sinking Ships, the Lost Heimat and Broken Taboos: Günter Grass and the Politics of Memory in Contemporary Germany." *Contemporary European History* 12/2 (2003): 147–81.

Moeller, Robert G. "Germans as Victims? Thoughts on a Post-Cold War History of World War II: Legacies." *History and Memory* 17/1–2 (Spring–Winter 2005): 145–94.

Moore, Brian Moore. *The Statement*. New York: Dutton, 1996.

Morris, James. "The Polish Terror: Spy Mania and Ethnic Cleansing in the Great Terror." *Europe-Asia Studies* 56/5 (2004): 751–66.

Moses, A. Dirk. *German Intellectuals and the Nazi Past*. Cambridge: Cambridge University Press, 2007.

Naimark, Norman H. "The Nazis and the 'East': Jedwabne's Circle of Hell." *Slavic Review* 61 (2002): 476–82.

Niven, Bill. *Facing the Nazi Past: United Germany and the Legacy of the Third Reich*. London: Routledge, 2002.

Niven, Bill, ed. *Germans as Victims: Remembering the Past in Contemporary Germany*. New York: Palgrave Macmillan, 2006.

Nolte, Ernst. *Three Faces of Fascism: Action Française, Italian Fascism, National Socialism*. Translated by Leila Vennewitz. New York: Holt, Rinehart and Winston, 1965.

Nolte, Ernst. *Deutschland und der kalte Krieg*. Munich: Piper, 1974.

Nolte, Ernst. *Der europäische Bürgerkrieg, 1917–1945: Nationalsozialismus und Bolschevismus*. Berlin: Propyläen Verlag, 1987.

Nossack, Hans Erich. *The End: Hamburg 1943*. Translated by Joel Agee. Chicago: University of Chicago Press, 2004.

Overy, Richard. *The Bombing War: Europe 1939–1945*. London: Penguin, 2014.

Pankowski, Rafal. *The Populist Radical Right in Poland: The Patriots*. London: Routledge, 2010.

Paxton, Robert O. *Vichy France: Old Guard and New Order, 1940–1944*. New York: Knopf, 1972.

Pfeifer, Douglas. Review of *Der Brand: Deutschland in Bombenkrieg 1940–1945*, by Jörg Friedrich. H-German, H-Net Reviews, November 2003. URL: http://www.h-net.org/reviews/showrev.php?id=8365.

Pohl, Dieter. "Die Holocaust Forschung und Goldhagens Thesen." *Vierteljahreshefte für Zeitgeschichte* 45 (1997): 12–48.

Poirot-Delpech, Bertrand. *Papon: un crime de bureau*. Paris: Stock, 1998.

Polonsky, Antony, and Joanna B. Michlic, eds. *The Neighbors Respond: The Controversy over the Jedwabne Massacre in Poland*. Princeton, NJ: Princeton University Press, 2004.

Porter-Szűcs, Brian. *Faith and Fatherland: Catholicism, Modernity, and Poland*. New York: Oxford University Press, 2011.

Porter-Szűcs, Brian. "The Triumph of National Communism." In *Poland's Memory Wars: Essays on Illiberalism*. Edited by Jo Harper. Budapest and New York: Central European University Press, 2018.

Prince, Cathryn J. *Death in the Baltic: The World War II Sinking of the Wilhelm Gustloff*. New York: Palgrave Macmillan, 2013.

Reid, Donald. "The Trial of Maurice Papon: History on Trial?" *French Politics and Society* 16 (1998): 62–79.

Rév, István. *Retroactive Justice: Prehistory of Post-Communism*. Stanford, CA: Stanford University Press, 2005.

Rieger, Bernard. "'Daniel in the Lion's Den?' The German Debate about Goldhagen's *Hitler's Willing Executioners*." *History Workshop Journal* 43 (1997): 226–33.

Röhl, Klaus Rainer. *Verbotene Trauer: Die vergessenen Opfer*. Munich: Universitas, 2002.

Rosenfeld, Gavriel D. "Deconstructivism and the Holocaust: Peter Eisenman's Memorial to the Murdered Jews of Europe." In *Probing the Ethics of Holocaust Culture*. Edited by Claudio Fogu, Wulf Kansteiner, and Todd Presner. Cambridge, MA: Harvard University Press, 2016,

Rosenhaft, Eve. "Facing Up to the Past—Again?" *Debatte: Journal of Contemporary Central and Eastern Europe* 5 (1997): 105–18.

Rossino, Alexander B. "Polish 'Neighbors' and German Invaders: Anti-Jewish Violence in the Białystok District during the Opening Weeks of Operation Barbarossa." *Polin: Studies in Polish Jewry* 16 (2003): 431–52.

Roth, John K. "Arno Mayer's Holocaust Revisions." *Holocaust and Genocide Studies* 5 (1990): 217–21.

Rothberg, Michael. *Multidirectional Memory: Remembering the Holocaust in the Age of Decolonization*. Stanford, CA: Stanford University Press, 2009.

Rousso, Henry. *The Vichy Syndrome: History and Memory in France since 1944*. Translated by Arthur Goldhammer. Cambridge, MA: Harvard University Press, 1991.

Rousso, Henry. "What Historians Will Retain from the Last Trial of the Purge." In *Memory, the Holocaust, and French Justice: The Bousquet and Touvier Affairs*. Edited by Richard J. Golsan. Translated by Lucy Golsan and Richard J. Golsan. Hanover, NH: University Press of New England, 1996.

Rousso, Henry. *The Haunting Past: History, Memory, and Justice in Contemporary France*. Translated by Ralph Schoolcraft. Philadelphia: University of Pennsylvania Press, 2002.

Rozett, Robert. *Conscripted Slaves: Hungarian Forced Laborers on the Eastern Front during the Second World War*. Jerusalem: Yad Vashem, 2013.

Sadat, Leila Nadya. "The Legal Legacy of Maurice Papon." In *The Papon Affair: Memory and Justice on Trial*. Edited by Richard J. Golsan. New York and London: Routledge, 2000.

Safrian, Hans. *Eichmann's Men*. Translated by Ute Stargardt. Cambridge: Cambridge University Press, 2010.

Sands, Philippe. *East West Street: On the Origins of "Genocide" and "Crimes Against Humanity."* New York: Knopf, 2016.

Schirrmacher, Frank, ed. *Die Walser-Bubis Debatte: Eine Dokumentation*. Frankfurt: Suhrkamp, 1999.

Sebald, W. G. *On the Natural History of Destruction*. Translated by Anthea Bell. New York: Modern Library Paperback, 2004.

Shandley, Robert R., ed. *Unwilling Germans? The Goldhagen Debate*. Minneapolis: University of Minnesota Press, 1998.

Sharples, Caroline. *Postwar Germany and the Holocaust*. London: Bloomsbury, 2016.

Shore, Marci. "Conversing with Ghosts: Jedwabne, Żydokomuna, and Totalitarianism." *Kritika: Explorations in Russian and Eurasian History* 6/2 (2005): 345–74.

Sion, Brigitte. "Affective Memory, Ineffective Functionality: Experiencing Berlin's Memorial to the Murdered Jews of Europe." In *Memorialization in Germany since 1945*. Edited by Bill Niven and Chloe Paver. New York: Palgrave Macmillan, 2010.

Smith, Bradley F. *Reaching Judgment at Nuremberg*. New York: Basic Books, 1977.

Snyder, Timothy. "The Causes of Ukrainian-Polish Ethnic Cleansing 1943." *Past and Present* 179 (2003): 197–234.

Snyder, Timothy. *The Reconstruction of Nations: Poland, Ukraine, Lithuania, Belarus, 1569–1999*. New Haven, CT: Yale University Press, 2003.

Snyder, Timothy. *Bloodlands: Europe between Hitler and Stalin*. New York: Basic Books, 2010.

Snyder, Timothy. *Black Earth: The Holocaust as History and Warning*. New York: Tim Duggan Books, 2015.

Soros, George, and Gregor Peter Schmitz, "'The EU Is on the Verge of Collapse'—An Interview." *New York Review of Books*, February 11, 2016.

Stargardt, Nicholas. *The German War: A Nation Under Arms, 1939–1945*. New York: Basic Books, 2015.

Steinlauf, Michael C. *Bondage to the Dead: Poland and the Memory of the Holocaust*. Syracuse, NY: Syracuse University Press, 1997.

Stola, Darius. "Jedwabne: Revisiting the Evidence and Nature of the Crime." *Holocaust and Genocide Studies* 17/1 (2003): 139–52.

Subotić, Jelana. *Yellow Star, Red Star: Holocaust Remembrance after Communism*. Ithaca, NY: Cornell University Press, 2019.

Suess, Dietmar. Review of *Brandstätten: Der Anblick des Bombenkrieges*, by Jörg Friedrich. H-German, H-Net Reviews, November 2004. URL: http://www.h-net.org/reviews/showrev.php?id=10004.

Taylor, Frederick. *Dresden, Tuesday February 13, 1945*. New York: HarperCollins, 2004.

Taylor, Telford. *The Anatomy of the Nuremberg Trials: A Personal Memoir*. New York: Knopf, 1992.

Thiele, Hans-Günter, ed. *Die Wehrmachtausstellung: Dokumentation eine Kontroverse.* Bremen: Edition Temmen, 1997.

Todorov, Tzvetan. "The Touvier Trial." In *Memory, the Holocaust, and French Justice: The Bousquet and Touvier Affairs.* Edited by Richard J. Golsan. Translated by Lucy Golsan and Richard J. Golsan. Hanover, NH: University Press of New Hampshire, 1996.

Torpey, John. "Introduction: Habermas and the Historians." *New German Critique* 44 (1988): 5–24.

Uhl, Heidemarie. "Interpreting the 'War of Annihilation': Responses to the Exhibition 'Crimes of the Wehrmacht: Dimensions of a War of Annihilation, 1941 to 1944' When Staged in Vienna in 2002." In *The Discursive Construction of History: Remembering the Wehrmacht's War of Annihilation.* Edited by Hannes Heer, Walter Manochek, Alexander Pollak, and Ruth Wodak. Translated by Steven Fligelstone. New York: Palgrave Macmillan, 2008.

Vági, Zoltán, László Csősz, and Gábor Kádár, eds. *The Holocaust in Hungary: Evolution of a Genocide.* Lanham, MD: AltaMira, 2013.

Vernichtungskrieg: Verbrechen der Wehrmacht 1941 bis 1944: Ausstellungskatalog. Hamburg: Hamburger Edition, 1996.

Vidal-Naquet, Pierre. *Assassins of Memory: Essays on the Denial of the Holocaust.* Translated by Jeffrey Mehlman. New York: Columbia University Press, 1992.

Violet, Bernard. *Le dossier Papon.* Paris: Flammarion, 1997.

Walser, Martin. "Experiences while Composing a Sunday Speech: The Peace Prize Speech" (1998). In *The Burden of the Past: Martin Walser on Modern German Identity and Texts, Contexts, and Commentary.* Translated by Thomas A. Kovach. Rochester, NY: Camden House, 2008.

Wehler, Hans-Ulrich. "Wie ein Stachel im Fleisch." In *Ein Volk von Mördern? Die Dokumentation zur Goldhagen Kontroverse um die Rolle der Deutschen im Holocaust.* Edited by Julius H. Schoeps. Hamburg: Hoffmann and Campe, 1997.

Westermann, Edward B. "Hitler's Uniformed Police on the Eastern Front: The Reich's Secret Soldiers, 1941–1942." *War in History* 3 (1996): 309–29.

Westermann, Edward B. "'Ordinary Men' or 'Ideological Soldiers'? Police Battalion 310 in Russia, 1942." *German Studies Review* 21 (1998): 41–68.

Wexler, Leila Sadat. "The Interpretation of the Nuremberg Principles by the French Court of Cassation: From Touvier to Barbie and Back Again." *The Columbia Journal of Transnational Law* 32 (1994): 289–380.

Wexler, Leila Sadat. "Reflections on the Trial of Vichy Collaborator Paul Touvier for Crimes against Humanity in France." *Law and Social Inquiry* 20 (Winter 1995): 191–221.

Wiedmer, Caroline. *The Claims of Memory: Representations of the Holocaust in Contemporary Germany and France.* Ithaca, NY: Cornell University Press, 1999.

Wieviorka, Annette. "France and Trials for Crimes against Humanity." In *Lives in Law.* Edited by Austin Sarat, Lawrence Douglas, and Martha Merrill Umphrey. Ann Arbor: University of Michigan Press, 2002.

Williams, Thomas Chatterton. "The French Origins of 'You Will Not Replace Us.'" *New Yorker*, December 4, 2017.
Wise, Michael Z. *Capital Dilemma: Germany's Search for a New Architecture of Democracy*. New York: Princeton Architectural Press, 1998.
Wise, Michael Z. "Totem and Taboo: The New Berlin Struggle to Build a Holocaust Memorial." *Lingua Franca: The Review of Academic Life* 8/9 (December/January 1999): 38–46.
Wood, Nancy. "Crimes or Misdemeanors? Memory on Trial in Contemporary France." *French Cultural Studies* 5 (1994): 1–21.
Young, James E. *The Texture of Memory: Holocaust Memorials and Meaning*. New Haven, CT: Yale University Press, 1993.
Young, James E. *At Memory's Edge: After-Images of the Holocaust in Contemporary Art and Architecture*. New Haven, CT: Yale University Press, 2000.
Young, James E. "Peter Eisenman's Design for the Berlin Memorial for the Murdered Jews of Europe: A Juror's Report in Three Parts." In *(Re)Visualizing National History: Museums and National Identities in the New Millennium*. Edited by Robin Ostow. Toronto: University of Toronto Press, 2008.
Zaoui, Michel. "Crimes contre l'humanité, conférence de Maître Michel Zaoui." http://www.cercleshoah.org/spip.php?article38.
Zaoui, Michel. *Mémoires de justice: Barbie, Touvier, Papon*. Paris: Seuil, 2009.
Zerofsky, Elisabeth. "Memory Politics: Does Poland's Government Want to Rewrite the Country's Past?" *New Yorker*, July 30, 2018.
Zerofsky, Elisabeth. "Viktor Orbán's Far-Right Vision for Europe." *New Yorker*, January 14, 2019.
Zubrzycki, Geneviève. *The Crosses of Auschwitz. Nationalism and Religion in Post-Communist Poland*. Chicago: University of Chicago Press, 2006.
Zuccotti, Susan. *The Holocaust, the French, and the Jews*. New York: Basic Books, 1993.

Index

Locators followed by "n." indicate endnotes

Action Française 67
Aftermath (*Pokłosie*) (film) 100–2
Algerian immigrants, FLN 13–14, 109 n.21
Algerian War (1958) 13, 15
Allied bombing campaign 2, 46, 57
Allies 3, 7–8, 26, 54, 56, 59, 88–9, 105
Alternative für Deutschland (AfD) 1, 105
Améry, Jean 57
Andersch, Alfred 57
annihilation principle 60
antifascism (Communist authorities) 1
anti-Semitism 1, 3, 19, 33, 36, 66, 86, 95, 98–101, 105–6
    commitment to fighting (Hollande) 23
    in Hungary 87, 89
    and Islamophobia 94
    of Milice 11
area bombing 55
Arrow Cross Party 89–91
Assize Court 108 n.12

Barbie, Klaus 8
    crimes against humanity 9
    as Klaus Altmann 8
    life imprisonment 9
    and Touvier's crimes 10
    trial 9–10
Barre, Raymond 6
Bartov, Omer 41
Baruch, Marc Olivier, *Servir l'État* 18–19
Bergen-Belsen concentration camp memorial site 46
Berlin Holocaust memorial. *See* Memorial to the Murdered Jews of Europe (Berlin)
Berlin Wall (1989), fall of 1
Bikont, Anna 97, 99–100
    The Crime and the Silence 97–8
Bild-Zeitung 59

Bitburg controversy 45–6, 115 n.2
Blum, Léon 6
Bolshevism 70
    vs. Nazism 65, 68
bombings 54–7, 59. *See also specific attacks*
Bousquet, René 6, 18
Browning, Christopher 27–32, 81
    Ordinary Men 27, 33, 36
Brunner, Alois 111 n.48
Bubis, Ignatz 46–7, 49
Bundestag 39–40, 105

Camus, Renaud 106
Central Agency for the State Administrations of Justice 31
Charlie Hebdo 94
Chirac, Jacques 5–6, 23
Christian democracy 93–4
Christian Democratic Union (CDU) 39–40, 52
Christian Social Union (CSU) 39
Churchill, Winston 7, 54, 59
Civic Platform (Poland) 96
"civilian populations" 9
"Civilization and Barbarism" project 37
crimes against humanity 6–8, 46, 108 n.13
    Barbie 9
    inhumane acts and persecutions 10
    Papon 6–8, 12
    Touvier 9–10
Crimes of the Wehrmacht: Dimensions of a War of Annihilation 1941 to 1944 42
criminal organizations 25, 37
Czop, Ireneusz 101

Dagerman, Stig 58
de Gaulle, Charles 13
Dershowitz, Alan 102
Der Spiegel 38, 42

Deutsches Historisches Museum 43, 50
Die Zeit 34–5, 38, 65, 69
Döblin, Alfred 58
Douglas, Lawrence 9
Dresden attack 56–7, 60, 119 n.60
Duda, Andrzej 103

Edelman, Marek 99
Eichmann, Adolf 88–9
Einaudi, Jean-Luc, *La bataille de Paris: 17 octobre 1961* 14–15, 109 n.21
Eisenman, Peter 50–3
emigration 75, 86
ethno-nationalism 3
exhibition
    double occupation, story of 90, 124 n.13
    Hungarian Holocaust, museum 89
    at Topography of Terror 50
    Wehrmacht 36–43, 114 n.51
extermination (Jews) 1–2, 6, 9, 26, 35–8, 41–2, 48, 52, 60–2, 65, 67–8, 71, 78, 80–3, 101, 105
    Auschwitz 68, 87
    Hungary 85–6, 88, 92
    in Jedwabne 96, 99–100
    in Józefów 29–30
    in Kielce 85–6
    in Kraków 85
    Kristallnacht 16, 76
    Łomazy 30–1
    in Minsk and Riga 28
    in Poland 29, 32, 82, 86
    in Serbia 37, 88
    systematic 10, 27
    Treblinka 31, 61, 119 n.60

fascism and communism (East/West Germany) 1–2
Fest, Joachim 67, 71
Fidesz 91–3, 95
Final Solution 2, 10, 25, 33, 78, 80–2, 88, 92
Finding Commission 50–2
First World War 26, 28, 45–6
Fischer, Joshka 52
forced labor service 19, 77, 88, 124 n.10
Foundation for Polish Science 71
France
    anti-refugee backlash 16

colonial past, excavating 12–15
deportation of Jews (*see* Jews, deportation)
Fifth Republic 6
Fourth Republic 6
Gayssot law 102
    legal procedure 108 n.12
principle of state continuity 5
Resistance 5, 8–9, 19
Third Republic 16–17
Frank, Hans 80
Frankfurter Allgemeine Zeitung 43, 67
Frei, Norbert 34
Freiburg Military Archive 38
Freikorps 26
Friedländer, Saul, *Nazi Germany and the Jews* 3, 68–70, 78, 80–2
Friedrich, Jörg 46, 54, 57, 118 n.32
    Brandstätten (*Sites of Fire*) 60–1
    Das Gesetz des Krieges (*The Law of War*) 59
    Der Brand (*The Fire*) 2, 46, 59–61
Front Libération Nationale (FLN) 13–14
Front National (Rassemblement National) 105
Furet, François 68

Gaulaud, Alexander 105
Gaullist 6
Gauweiler, Peter 39
Gazeta Wyborcza 97
genocide. *See* extermination (Jews)
Gerlach, Christian 80–1
German occupation 16, 28–9, 65–6, 71, 79, 88, 90, 92
German police forces, branches 26
Germany 44
    and anti-Semitism 3, 33, 98
    criminal Nazis and normal Germans 35–6
    guilt for National Socialism 1–2
    memorial 49
    policies of mass murder 71
    suffering revisited 54–61
    unification 2
Gestapo-SD 25
Giscard d'Estaing, Valéry 6, 12
Glemp, Józef 99
Globocnik, Odilo 29

Goldhagen, Daniel Jonah 3
  Democracy Prize 36
  fault with Browning's interpretation 32
  Hitler's Willing Executioners: Ordinary Germans and the Holocaust 2, 26–36
Grass, Günter, *Krebsgang* (*Crabwalk*) 62–4, 120 n.67
Great Terror 75–6
Green Party 40, 52
Gross, Jan, *Neighbors* 96–100

Habermas, Jürgen 53, 65–6
Hamburg firebombing. *See* Operation Gomorrah
Hamburg Institute for Social Research 37
Harris, Arthur 55
Heer, Hannes 39
Heidegger, Martin 67
Henriot, Philippe 10–11
Herbert, Ulrich 44
Heydrich, Reinhard 26
Hillgruber, Andreas 62, 64
  Zweierlei Untergang: Die Zerschlagung des Deutschen Reiches und das Ende des europäischen Judentums (*Two Sorts of Collapse: The Destruction of the German Reich and the End of European Jewry*) 62
Himmler, Heinrich 26–7, 29, 65, 79, 82
Hiroshima and Nagasaki, atomic attacks 56
Historikerstreit 65–70
Hitler, Adolf 10, 16, 26–7, 33, 36–7, 39, 42, 44–5, 48, 54, 59–60, 62–7, 69–71, 76, 78, 80–2, 89
  plans for Eastern Europe 81
  utopias 78–9
Hiwis 30–1
Hofstadter, Richard, concept of paranoid style 106
Hollande, François 15, 23
Holocaust 1, 3, 23, 47, 52–3, 61, 81–2, 106. *See also* extermination (Jews)
Holocaust Memorial Center (Budapest) 89–90
Holocaust Memorial Museum in Washington, D. C. 31
Horthy, Miklós 88–9, 92–4
  numerus clausus law 87
House of Terror 90, 124 n.13
  "Farewell" 91

Hungarian Holocaust, museum 89
Hungarian Revolution (1956) 86
Hungary 1, 3, 16, 105
  anti-Jewish demonstrations 85
  foreign policy 88
  German occupation of 88
  history of (1944 to 1989) 91
  past, denying 87–95
Hunger Plan 78–9, 123 n.55
hunger zone 79

Ignatiew, Radosław 97–8
immigrants/immigration 106
  Algerian 13
  to Israel 86
  zero tolerance for 94
Indicting Chamber of the Paris Court of Appeals 10, 108 n.12
Information Center 52–3
Institute of National Remembrance 97
International Holocaust Remembrance Day 102
international law 7, 37, 42
International Military Tribunal 7–8

Jabłonski, Dariusz 101
Jäckel, Eberhard 34, 47, 65
Jackson, Robert 7
  prosecution, statement 25
Janssen, Karl-Heinz 38
Jeismann, Michael 43
Jews 2, 20, 27–8, 45, 49, 66, 68, 70, 82, 87, 91, 97. *See also* extermination (Jews)
  census of (occupied/unoccupied zones) 17–18
  deportation 2, 6, 9, 18–22, 27, 29, 42, 80, 85–6, 89–90
  elimination 33, 42–3, 75, 78, 80
  incarcerated in Lyon prison 8
  Lublin plan 80
  memorial (*see specific Jews memorials*)
  Vél d'Hiv roundups (1942) 5–6, 23
  victimization by compatriots 1
Jobbik 93, 95
Judt, Tony 1

Kaczyński, Jarosław 95–6
Klarsfeld, Serge 9, 15

Klemperer, Victor 69
  I Will Bear Witness: A Diary of the Nazi Years 1933–1945 121 n.19
  LTI (*Lingua tertii imperii*, 1947) 69–70
Kohl, Helmut 39, 45–6, 49, 51–2
Kollwitz, Käthe, "Mother with her Dead Son" 46
"Kraft durch Freude" ("Strength through Joy") program 62–3
Kristallnacht pogroms 16, 76
Kwaśniewski, Aleksander 100

Lauterpacht, Hersch 7
Law and Justice (Poland) 96, 102–3, 105
law-free zone 42
laws of war 42
Le Canard enchaîné 12
le grand remplacement (great replacement) 106
Leguay, Jean 6
Lemkin, Raphael 75
Le Monde 6
Le Pen, Jean-Marie 105
Le Pen, Marine 1, 105
liberal democracy 94–5

Macron, Emmanuel 15
Manstein, Erich von 42
mass extermination 61. *See also* extermination (Jews)
memorial, creating 47–54. *See also specific memorials*
  series of public colloquia 49
  victims of fascism and militarism 45
  "victims of war and tyranny" 45
Memorial to the Murdered Jews of Europe (Berlin) 2, 46–7, 49, 52–3, 65, 105
In Memory of the Victims of the German Occupation 92
Merkel, Angela 95
Mitterand, François 6, 12
mobilization of October 17 13
Mommsen, Hans 34–5
Moulin, Jean 8
murder of Jews. *See* extermination (Jews)
Musial, Bodgan 41
Musiał, Stanisláw 100

Nagy, Imre 91
National Socialism 2, 44, 67–8
  crimes 1, 38, 68
Naumann, Michael 52
Nazi Germany 3, 6, 9, 12, 28, 34, 37, 46–7, 60–2, 68, 76, 78, 82, 87–8, 90, 102, 105
  depravity of 69
  Generalplan Ost 78–9
  genocidal policy 96 (*see also* extermination (Jews))
  Germanizing 76
  linguistic practices 70
  social significance of 63
Nazism, Bolshevism *vs.* 65, 68
neo-Nazi National Democratic Party 39
Neue Wache (New Guardhouse) 45
  rededication 45–6
Nickels, Christa 40
1945 (film) 85
NKVD 41, 75, 77
Nolte, Ernst 65–9, 71
  anti-Soviet animus 3
  Der europäische Bürgerkrieg (*The European Civil War*) 70
  Der Faschismus in seiner Epoche (*Three Faces of Fascism*) 67–8
  Deutschland und der kalte Krieg (*Germany and the Cold War*) 67
  "The Past That Will Not Pass" 67
Nossack, Hans Erich, *Der Untergang* (*The End: Hamburg 1943*) 59
Nuremberg Laws 87

Oberg, Karl 18
October 17 massacre 13, 109 n.21
Open Society Foundation 95
Operation Barbarossa 26, 33, 79–82, 96
Operation Gomorrah 55–6, 59
Operation Tannenberg 77
Orbán, Viktor 91–3, 105
  Christian democracy 93–4
  ethnic and religious nationalism 95
  "illiberal democracy" 1, 92, 96
Orphuls, Marcel
  Hotel Terminus (1988) 9
  The Sorrow and the Pity 5

Papon, Maurice 2, 6, 14, 19–20, 109 n.21
  to combat terrorism 13–14
  crimes against humanity 6–8, 12
  fifty-seventh session trial 21–2
  hegemonic political ideology (Nazis) 12, 22
  imprisonment 22
  North African possessions (France) 12
  personal responsibility 15
  as prefect of police 13
  protectorate of Morocco 13
Pasikowski, Władysław 100. *See also Aftermath (Pokłosie)* (film)
Paxton, Robert O. 16, 18–19
  Vichy France: Old Guard and New Order, 1940-1944 5
Pétain, Philippe 10, 17
Poirot-Delpech, Bertrand, *Papon: un crime de bureau* 16–22
Poland 1, 3, 16, 27, 43, 71, 95, 105
  Civic Platform 96
  decapitation of Polish society 77
  deportations 76–7
  emigrants 75
  honor, defending 95–102
  international reputation 87
  Law and Justice 96, 102–3, 105
  slaughter of Jews in 29, 32, 82, 86
  slave laborers 78
"Polish-death-camps amendment" 102
Pompidou, Georges 10
POW camp 27

Reagan, Ronald 45–6
Red Army 38–9, 44, 62, 71, 79–80, 89, 91
Red-Green coalition 52
Reemtsma, Jan Philipp 39, 41
refugee crisis 3, 16, 96
Reichenau, Walter von 42
Reserve Police Battalion 101 27–32, 34
Reynaud, Paul 17
Roosevelt, Franklin Delano 7
Rosh, Lea 47–8, 65
Rundstedt, Gerd von 42
Russian Revolution 68, 72
Russo-Polish War (1919–20) 75

Sabatier, Maurice 6, 21–2
Schinkel, Karl Friedrich 45

Schröder, Gerhard 52
Sebald, W. G. 54, 59, 119 n.60
  Luftkrieg und Literatur (*The Air War and Literature*) 46
  On the Natural History of Destruction 57–8
Second World War 7, 42, 45, 70–1, 81, 87–9
series of public colloquia 49
Serra, Richard 50–1
Seventeenth Chamber of the Paris Correctional Tribunal 15
Shily, Otto 39
Siedler Verlag 34
Sinti and Roma 27–8, 47–8
Six-Day War 86
slaughter of Jews. *See* extermination (Jews)
Slitinsky, Michel 11–12
Snyder, Timothy 3, 65, 73–82
  Bloodlands 65, 70–1, 83
  Eastern Europe, populations 3, 87
Sobieski, Jan 96
Social Democratic Party (SPD) 39, 52
Soros, George 95
Soviet Union, German invasion of. *See* Operation Barbarossa
SS 25, 28, 46, 88, 119 n.60
Stalin, Joseph 7, 37, 65–6, 74–6, 81–2, 86
  "Dizzy with Success" 72
  record of mass murder 71
  unprecedented agricultural experiment (Ukraine) 72
Statut des juifs 17
strategic bombing surveys 54
Stuhr, Maciej 101
Szálasi, Ferenc 89

Tessenow, Heinrich 45–6
Third Reich 2, 10, 16, 28, 38, 59, 68, 102, 121 n.19
Tokyo, fire-bombing 56
Touvier, Paul 9–10
  crimes against humanity 9–10
  green notebook 11
  penalties 10
  sentenced to life 11
Trapp, Wilhelm 28–30
Treaty of Trianon 88, 93

Truman, Harry 7
Tusk, Donald 96

Ukraine
  "the breadbasket of Europe" 72
  collectivization of agriculture 65, 72–4, 79, 81
  Holodomor 74
  kulaks 72–3, 76
  New Economic Policy 72
Ullrich, Volker 35
Ungváry, Krisztián 41
United Nations convention (1948) 74
Unite the Right 106
Unsere Mütter, unsere Väter (Generation War) 43

Veesenmayer, Edmund 89
Vél d'Hiv roundups (1942) 5–6, 23, 105
Vernichtungskrieg: Verbrechen der Wehrmacht 1941 bis 1944. See War of Annihilation: Crimes of the Wehrmacht, 1941–1944
Versailles Treaty 26
  conscription in open defiance of 26
Vichy regime 2, 5–6, 9–10, 16, 105
  anti-Jewish measures 18
  anti-Semitic policy 11
The Vietnam Memorial in Washington, D.C. 53

Walser, Martin 47, 53, 57
  intellectual arson 47
war crimes 8–9, 12, 42–3, 46
War of Annihilation: Crimes of the Wehrmacht, 1941–1944 2, 26, 37–8, 114 n.51
Wehler, Hans-Ulrich 34
Wehrmacht, crimes of 36–43, 59, 71
Weimar Republic 45
Weinmiller, Gesine 50
Weis, Ernst 26–7
Weiss, Peter 57
Weizmann, Chaim 68
Weizsäcker, Richard von 46
World Jewish Congress 68
Wprost 101

xenophobia 19

Yad Vashem 47, 52
Yezhov, Nicolai 75
Young, James E. 49–51

Zaoui, Michel 21–2
Zentrale Stelle der Landesjustizverwaltungen. *See* Central Agency for the State Administrations of Justice
Zionism 86

www.ingramcontent.com/pod-product-compliance
Lightning Source LLC
Chambersburg PA
CBHW061842300426
44115CB00013B/2480